THE FRIARY
LEARNING CENTRE

ONE MONTH LOAN

Deaf Again

Cover design courtesy of
Damara Goff Paris,
AGO Gifts and Publications

*In the interest of privacy, some names in this
book have been changed.*

Published by: Handwave Publications
1201 Bethlehem Pike
Suite 105
North Wales, PA 19454-2157

ISBN: 0-9657460-0-3

Catalog Card Number: 99-091839

Dedication

In loving memory of Linda Baine,
who taught me how to be Deaf

and

In loving memory of Martin J. Bronenberg,
who taught me how to be anything I wanted to be

Acknowledgments

Heartfelt thanks to my parents and grandparents, for all the love and support.
To my wife Melanie, for putting up with all the insanity.

To Teresa Coates, for helping me get started.
To DeafNation, for giving me the opportunity to grow as a writer.
To Damara Goff Paris, for her amazing innovation and creativity.

To Lisa Bain, for her very helpful feedback.
To Sam Scott, for his incredible encouragement.

To Fran, Pat, Allen, Frank, Roger, Bill and Ruth – teachers extraordinaire.
To Michael P. Ralph, Patty Saar and Lisa Santomen, the best colleagues and friends a guy could ask for.
To Arlene Kim Weinstock... what, lunch duty again?

To Audrey, Dragan, Jeff and Cheryl – for tolerating the intolerable. Bless you.
To my new family in Canada. Look what you got yourselves into.
To Colby, Neil, Sarah and the rest of the 5-F club. See you on Friday.
To Jeff, Vijay, Derek and Jason: We're still the Family.

Introduction

The hardest fight a man has to fight is to live in a world where every single day someone is trying to make you someone you do not want to be —-
                                                        e.e. cummings

Trying to be a hearing person can be an extremely difficult fight, especially when your audiogram is free-falling towards the depths of profound deafness. As a hearing youngster who gradually went hard of hearing and then eventually deaf, I struggled all the way through my high school years trying to hang on to my hearing persona. What makes this really odd is that the whole time this charade was going on, Deaf culture was always there for me, right under my nose: both of my parents are Deaf.

But as quickly as I was born into Deaf culture, I was taken away from it. When my hearing loss was initially diagnosed, medical professionals took an entirely pathological approach, emphasizing hearing aids and speech therapy. Since they did not recognize or understand Deaf culture, they frowned upon the use of sign language. These specialists preached a skewed version of the old "it's a hearing world" philosophy, somehow convincing my hearing relatives and teachers to discourage my Deaf parents from using sign language with me. It was a vain attempt at holding on to what little residual hearing and speech I had left. This experience left me with the impression that deafness was a horrendous condition which needed to be fixed, or at least covered up. Consequently, I felt obligated to spend the next several years of my life trying to pass myself off as a hearing person. I spent those years living my life as someone I thought I should be, instead of as who I really was.

Inevitably, I would wake up. A series of fateful events turned my life around to the point where I realized it was okay to be Deaf. It took twenty-three years to come to that realization, twenty-three years of struggling with my identity. Instead of trying to deny or fix deafness, I found that I could be Deaf again, and grew tremendously from the experience. As opposed to overcoming deafness, this book expresses the joys of finding deafness.

While putting together a rough draft of what eventually became this book, I also noticed that a number of spiritual issues repeatedly came to surface. I began to realize that in its own strange way, deafness has been a spiritual blessing for me. Dealing with deafness is a struggle, yes, but it's also a struggle that has enabled me to search for meaning in life from a unique perspective. An old Zen saying applies here: *empty your cup so that it may be filled.* Deafness emptied my cup. The void in one area of my life allowed me to have enriching experiences in others. Deaf Again is thus a deeply introspective account of the challenges faced in coming to terms with hearing loss.

As you will see in upcoming chapters, there is no hard-core, etched-in-stone definition of what constitutes a deaf person. There is just too much diversity out there. There are deaf people who consider themselves culturally Deaf (caps intended), embracing American Sign Language as their own language. Then there are oralists, deaf people who favor speech over sign language. There are also those who are somewhat in between, using whatever combination of speech and sign language they are comfortable with. All of these people have many incredibly diverse backgrounds. Deaf people who went to residential schools. Deaf people who went to mainstream schools which had special programs for deaf students. Deaf people who went to hearing schools alone without any deaf peers or assistance. Deaf people who are prelingually deaf, hard of hearing or late-deafened. Deaf people with hearing parents, deaf people with deaf parents, and so on. All of these people may have varying opinions of what deafness means.

What makes *Deaf Again* unique is the fact that I have personally seen deafness from many perspectives: hearing toddler, hard-of-hearing child, deaf adolescent and culturally Deaf adult. Throughout all of this, I saw firsthand the philosophical war of deafness the culture versus deafness the pathology. This book is intended to show an up-close viewpoint of each side, as seen through the eyes of someone who has been on both sides of the fence. Whatever your own background may be, I hope that you can find stories in here that you can relate to... and stories that you can learn from. So empty your cup, and enjoy the journey.

Prologue

It was another dreary Saturday morning, and I was packing the shelves as usual in the supermarket where I worked part-time. I hated working the Saturday morning shift because it meant getting up at 5:30 in the morning, usually with a throbbing hangover. Every weekend, it was the same old story. My college friends would stop by on Friday night, informing me of a great party taking place. I would politely decline, pointing out that I had to work early the next morning. They would rant and rave about what a wimp I was, and I would eventually cave in and go along with them. They would proceed to have a great time... and I would pretend to. After all, I was deaf as a post and had no idea of what was being said around me. Sure, with my residual hearing and respectable speech ability, I managed to pull off a few successful one-on-one conversations with certain people. Unfortunately, I was always lost in group discussions and was generally bored out of my mind a great majority of the time.

Out of this boredom, I would always wind up reaching for more beers than my friends were drinking. By midnight, I would have quite a buzz going. By three a.m., I would be flat-out drunk. By four a.m., I would be crawling into bed (if I made it that far). By six-thirty, I would be cursing under my breath as I punched in for work.

This particular Saturday was no different. Saturday was diaper day, when a whole truckload of diapers got dropped off at the store in the wee hours of the morning. They were waiting for me when I trudged in with bloodshot eyes and a pounding headache. As I loaded them onto a cart to be wheeled out and packed on the shelves, it felt like the veins in my head were going to burst.

By nine a.m., the diapers were done and it was time to do the really mundane stuff. I worked in the general merchandise section, ordering and packing out non-perishable goods such as school supplies, personal hygiene products, hardware, toys and various clothing items. Each time I worked a shift, customers who needed help finding whatever it was that they were looking for would interrupt me. Normally I didn't mind, so long as they were regular customers who knew me. I dreaded having to talk to new customers who didn't understand that I was deaf. It was always an awkward struggle. The regulars knew me well enough to make sure they spoke clearly, and I was familiar with their speech patterns after seeing the same faces every week for three years.

The new customers, however, were always an adventure of foul-ups, bleeps and blunders. One man asked me repeatedly where he could find a certain product, and he began to shout in my ear when I told him I was deaf. I never got to explain that he needed to look me in the eye and enunciate his words more clearly for me to lip-read... because he stormed off, muttering angrily. Another man, whose question I successfully understood and answered, asked me what country I was from as I apparently had an interesting accent. When I told him that it was just a result of my not being able to hear my voice because I was deaf, his eyes widened.

"Ohhhhh," he said, backing away. "I see." He nodded awkwardly, waved goodbye, and made a hasty retreat. From this experience, I learned to simply say,

"Excuse me, I'm a bit hard of hearing... could you speak a little slower for me?" This always got a favorable response. For whatever reason, the word "deaf" seemed to freak out some people.

And then there were people who freaked *me* out. On one occasion, I had turned around just in time to see a woman throwing a tantrum at me.

"Why, I never... (unintelligible)... such a rude man... (unintelligible)... I oughta —" I could only shrug helplessly. Ten minutes later, this woman returned with the store manager and pointed at me. He smiled, made a comment or two, and all of a sudden this woman grabbed my arm and began to apologize profusely.

"I'm so sorry... I didn't know you were *death*." Apparently, she thought I was ignoring her when she asked me a question behind my back. She just couldn't see that I was *death*. Whatever. At least I liked her better than the guy with the walrus mustache. Nothing, except perhaps grabbing him in a headlock and shaving the fur off his face, could have helped me there. I explained to him that I couldn't hear, and he patiently repeated his question slowly several times... but that rug on his upper lip just wouldn't allow me to get one word. In exasperation, I just sighed and said,

"Aisle twenty-seven." Never mind that there were only twenty-six aisles in the store. It was his problem. Let *him* figure it out.

But today, there was one customer who would change everything for me. My attitude, my confidence, my job, my future, my life, *everything*. I was stocking the shelves with dental floss when someone politely tapped me on the shoulder. I turned around thinking *what is it now...* and was very surprised to be greeted by a woman who was asking me something in fluent sign language.

"Hi, I'm Linda Baine... remember me?" Indeed I did... she worked at the Pennsylvania School for the Deaf, and I remembered meeting her when she was interpreting a community event I attended a few years earlier. Linda was a hearing woman, but she signed so smoothly she looked Deaf herself. It was such a relief to be able to converse effortlessly with someone after all those adventures with the other customers.

"Sure, I remember you," I said. "How have you been doing?"

"Just great," Linda began. "I just got promoted to Coordinator of Residential Education... which is why I'm here. Listen, we have an opening for a dorm supervisor at the school. I'm telling you, it would be the perfect opportunity for you..."

My life would never, ever be the same.

Chapter 1

On the afternoon of October 12th, 1966, a very pregnant Sherry Drolsbaugh was wheeled into the delivery room accompanied by her husband, Don. As she recalls, she was strapped into place. Yes, they tied her down. Whether that was common practice back then or if it was just because Sherry was hysterically screaming for morphine, I'm not sure. This was taking place at the Albert Einstein Medical Center near downtown Philadelphia, one of the best hospitals in the city. However, whatever skills doctors had back in the 1960's, even the best of them knew very little about deafness. For my mother and father, both Deaf, this set the stage for a harrowing experience.

As Sherry was strapped down, she gestured to one of the nurses, requesting that they free one of her hands. This way, she explained, she would be able to communicate with her husband through sign language. Presumably, she would use that hand to tell him what a bastard he was for getting her in this predicament in the first place, and maybe even grab his throat if the pain got too unbearable. Ever the good sport, Don stuck with her throughout the whole ordeal.

And what an ordeal it was! Right off the bat, there were some, uh, technical difficulties. As Sherry explains it, the nurse took a needle that was to administer epidural and applied it to her backside. It was taped on so that it would continuously administer some much-needed pain relief. However, as the whole procedure began, Sherry complained constantly that she was in pain. One of the nurses, getting in close for a good view of the whole show, leaned on her leg. Sherry yelped and signed furiously to Don:

"Tell the nurse to get her elbow off me!"

When Don relayed the message to the nurse, she shook her head and chuckled. She insisted there was no way Sherry could feel anything because of the epidural. The hospital staff kept working and Sherry eventually gave birth, screaming bloody murder the whole time. Finally, when the doctor began sewing up whatever it is that obstetricians are supposed to sew up, my mother couldn't take it anymore. She repeatedly complained about the excruciating pain that was becoming harder to tolerate. She begged the doctor to knock her out with a good old-fashioned general anesthetic... *anything* to get over the searing pain. Sighing, the doctor figured why not... might as well help her relax and get her to shut up, too. Everyone would be happy.

Unfortunately, this whole caper was far from over. As the anesthesia mask was placed over her nose and mouth, Sherry's eyes widened in horror. Choking, she realized *there was no air at all*. She was suffocating. Immediately she panicked, waving vigorously at the doctor and attending nurses. But since Sherry is prelingually deaf, she never has had the ability to speak clearly, and this communication barrier in the hospital almost proved to be deadly. The doctor and nurses immediately assumed that her muffled grunts and struggling were just more of her typical delivery room antics, so they didn't take it seriously. They smiled, reassured Sherry that everything was okay, and told her to just let the anesthetic do its work. They further restrained her and kept the mask firmly in place. In horror, my mother realized she was in a nightmare of a situation one would expect to find on *The Twilight Zone*.

Thinking quickly, Sherry raised the one hand that the nurse freed a little bit earlier and frantically began fingerspelling to Don.

"N-o a-i-r! N-o a-i-r!"

Alarmed and confused, Don looked around the operating room and saw that the anesthesia machine was not working. A pump that was supposed to be pumping was instead clamped shut, stuck in place. He grabbed the mask off Sherry's face and pointed out the defective equipment to the doctor, who gasped in both shock and embarrassment. He apologized and asked Sherry to "just hang in there" while he cut this, sewed that, and generally cleaned up the mess I had made on the way out. Don reinforced Sherry all the while, telling her to bear with the pain; the whole thing was almost over. Besides, all screw-ups notwithstanding, they were overjoyed to be the proud new parents of a healthy boy.

In the midst of all the "hey it's a boy!" congratulations, a nurse began to help Sherry off of the delivery room table and onto a gurney, so she could be whisked to her room. Immediately, the nurse spotted something on the table and gasped. There was a large, wet spot in the vicinity of the needle that was (supposedly) administering the epidural. Peeling off the tape that was holding the needle in place, the nurse found that it was bent off at an angle. It had been leaking off onto the table the whole time, instead of providing Sherry the painkilling relief she was begging for. No wonder she was screaming like crazy!

Sherry immediately noticed that there had been some kind of grim discovery. Panicking, she asked Don and the nurse what was wrong.

"Nothing at all, nothing at all, the baby is just fine," replied the nurse, speaking slowly so my parents could read her lips. Turning to Don, she said, "your wife is a very brave woman... she just had a natural childbirth, whether she knew it or not." Oh, she knew. Believe me, she knew.

Chapter 2

From that zany childbirth all the way up to the first grade, I had perfectly normal hearing. I think. I was able to acquire language the way hearing children usually do, through both auditory and visual input. I could have conversations on the phone with my hearing grandparents, and seemed to interact normally with other children my age. I attended kindergarten at the Henry H. Houston School in Philadelphia, and there was nothing out of the ordinary that anyone may have noticed.

However, I recall being confused at times during weekly music classes. There were moments when I felt something was not quite right whenever we sang songs together. When it was my turn or my group's turn to sing a line, I either missed my turn or babbled something incomprehensible. Sometimes I made up my own lines. I would sing about my gal who rode the boat outdoors with Al and Louie, and then I would wonder why everyone was looking at me so funny. I would shrug bewilderedly as the teacher corrected me — the actual words, she said, were "Michael row the boat ashore, hallelujah." Hey, I was only singing what I thought I heard. At that age, children are naturally very egocentric; I couldn't help but think that the other kids were receiving the same warped input as I was. I didn't really believe at the time that something might have been seriously wrong with me.

Finally, my weirdness was exposed for all to see on one fateful day in the first grade. It was time for our favorite weekly activity, Show 'n' Tell. As did any other student, I loved this part of class because it put me in the spotlight and enabled me to share my toys with everyone. This time, however, I was doomed. For some reason, my teacher decided to have one huge Show 'n' Tell activity featuring two first grade classes working together. Instead of the cozy atmosphere of twelve or so students sharing their favorite things, there were thirty kids packed in one big room. I felt lost. It was my first experience of complete disorientation; I realized I had no idea of what anyone was saying, or how I would know when it was my turn. And the worst was yet to come.

"Mark... you're up," said my teacher, Ms. Brown.

"Huh?"

"Mark, it's your turn... come on up."

I made my way up to the front, bringing the toy I knew would knock 'em dead: my GI Joe doll, dressed up in army fatigues. I even took good measure to toughen him up for class; I had seared off part of his scalp with a lit match, cut some scars in his face with a knife, and threw him around in the dirt. Anything for that rugged look, you know. No, I wasn't one of those sick kids who like to fry ants on the sidewalk with a magnifying glass, but hey, I wanted my GI Joe to look *tough*. No one would mess with him, and I would impress the class.

Immediately, though, I was in trouble. I was explaining how GI Joe survived several bombings, knife fights, attacks by hairy savages, and even that yecchy tea party thrown by the girl with the Barbie set. Whatever it was, Joe always got out alive. Then suddenly, a hand raised. One of the kids had a question, and it was a kid from the other first grade class. I had no idea who he was. Apparently, since I didn't know him, I wasn't familiar with his speech pattern. There was no way I could understand what he was saying in a crowded classroom, all those rows back. Thus began my coming out party, where all notions that I was a hearing boy went out the window.

"Where did you blsszth thsdke klsnolthng?"

"What?" I responded.

"Where'dublsthes tsjdkke gsjdngfhg?"

"WHAT??..." I was getting frustrated. At this point, Ms. Brown cut in to point out that my manners were inappropriate. She was trying to explain that instead of contorting my face and screaming "WHAT??", it would be more gentlemanly to politely raise my eyebrows and say "yes?" to the boy.

"Yes, what?" I asked Ms. Brown.

"Don't say what, say yes".

"WHAT?"

"Y-E-S. Yes."

"What was the question I'm saying yes to?"

"No, no, you say 'yes?' politely to him so he'll repeat the question." Shrugging, I looked back at the boy.

"Yes?"

"Where did blshdth thesjcl dlnfjthng?"

"WHAT????"

And so the verbal volleyball went on. I had no idea specifically that something was seriously wrong here; I only remember the wide-eyed looks I got from the whole classroom. *Something* was not right, but at this point, with my five-year old reasoning ability, it didn't quite hit me yet that I was going deaf.

Shortly after that fiasco in Show 'n' Tell, I found myself in my grandparents' apartment. Back in those days, the word "accessibility" didn't exist... there was no effective communication between the school and my deaf parents. Anytime a phone call had to be made, teachers would call my maternal grandparents, Martin and Rose, who were hearing. Inadvertently, for better and for worse, they wound up taking charge in terms of overseeing my progress in school.

On this infamous day, my grandfather summoned for me and asked me to sit down... he really needed to talk to me. I still remember vividly the worried look of concern on his face. Apparently, he must have got one of those "good news and bad news" phone calls from my teacher. The good news was "no, we don't think your grandson is crazy after all"... and the bad news was "instead, we think he has a significant hearing loss."

So now it was time for the truth to come out. My grandfather began making small conversation, nothing out of the ordinary. Suddenly, he asked what seemed to be an unusual question to me:

"Can you understand what I'm saying?"

"Yeah, sure..." I was perplexed. I couldn't see what the big deal was... and yet he looked so *worried*.

"Okay, now let's try it this way." My grandfather lifted his hand, covered his mouth, and began speaking.

"Howbout rhynow? Cnu erwt imsyng? Mrk, cnu unrandme?"

"What? Yes?"

My grandfather recoiled in shock. It just hit him, and very hard, that I had been reading lips all along. Up until that point, my residual hearing and speaking ability were just enough to cover up any indication of a hearing loss. Not anymore.

Now this is where it gets complicated. This one simple discovery, and the reaction to it, had a major impact on the path my life would take. For the first time, I understood that something was seriously wrong, and that *something was seriously wrong with me.* Let me make it clear, though, if it isn't already, that my grandparents both loved me so much that they would do anything to make my life the best for me. However, there was a paradox in the works here, a paradox I would not come to understand until more than twenty years later.

Fast-forwarding several years for just a moment here: it wasn't until I took a Psycho-social Aspects of Deafness course at Gallaudet University when I finally understood the dynamics of what went on when my grandparents discovered I was going deaf (doctors confirmed my grandfather's worst fears when they diagnosed a progressive sensorineural hearing loss). My teacher was discussing what is called "The Diagnostic Crisis" involving deafness. When hearing parents (in my case, grandparents) first learn that their child is deaf, it can be very overwhelming. It is a shock, a tremendous shock, and it sets off a reaction that is similar to the stages of grief (shock, denial, anger, depression, the whole works). The difference is, they are not grieving a dead person. They are grieving for someone who is very much alive, and in the process can greatly influence that person. When a deaf child sees hearing family going overboard over his or her newly diagnosed deafness, a lasting impression is made. As the parents are visibly upset and ship the kid off to every medical specialist they can find (even with the best intentions, hoping to find that one miracle cure), the child may perceive a different message:

Deafness is bad. I am deaf. I need to be fixed. I must be like them, no matter what, because deaf is bad.

The irony is, my grandparents were doing everything in their power to help me. They sent me to doctors, audiologists, speech therapists, everything but a witch doctor. Their actions were saying "we love you, we'll do anything to help you hear like normal people do." Unbeknownst to them, the mixed message I received was "we love you, but... deafness is a horrible condition, and we have to fix you."

What are the psychological implications of such a message? To me, it meant I had to deny who I really was, and had to pretend I was hearing. It meant I had to brownnose to hearing people, act like them, act like I understood them, and remove myself from anything associated with deafness. In other words, sign language was *verboten*. Many Deaf people to this day still ask me how it was possible for me to be raised this way, because my own parents are Deaf. Surely, they could have told everyone to back off and just leave me alone with my deafness. But my residual hearing and speech at the time were just so close to that of a hearing person (back then, I could still hold a decent phone conversation, even if sometimes I had to ask people to repeat things). If I had been born completely deaf, perhaps this would have been a totally different story. But I was so close. So my grandparents did everything in their power to hold on to whatever hearing and speech I had left, and hopefully find a way to improve on it.

In this frenzied quest for normal hearing, doctors and so-called experts bombarded us with the old "it's a hearing world" routine. This meant I needed to wear hearing aids and work on my speech at all times, never signing. The doctors told my hearing grandparents to make sure my Deaf parents didn't use sign language with me, because they felt it would cause me to lose my speech, a supposedly crucial element of my development. The experts had spoken, and that was that. So my parents would sign to each other, but tried mostly to use voice with me. Hence I grew up to be a very rare oddity in the Deaf world: a deaf child of Deaf parents who couldn't sign worth a damn until his mid-twenties.

This pathological approach to deafness is the hardest part of the book for me to write. Not because it was a difficult experience for me; quite the contrary, it was a learning experience. Yet I share it with some reluctance, for I know it must be painful for both my parents and my grandparents to read. I don't even *want* them to read it. To this day, my grandmother (on the rare occasions we have frank discussions about deafness) has still expressed feelings of remorse over something that was not her fault at all. Besides, how can you blame people for wanting what they truly believe is best for you? My grandmother has at various times remarked that "we were only doing what the doctors told us to do," and wonders if she made a huge, irreparable mistake. She did not.

While she and my grandfather were encouraging me to grow closer to the hearing world, they were also helping me go through the best educational programs in the state. Educational programs which by far blew away anything that any deaf program had to offer at the time (more on that later). If you ask me, the trade-off was worth it, and I owe my grandparents a ton of thanks. I would not have the literary skills to write this book in the first place were it not for their involvement in my educational endeavors.

Likewise, my own parents have at times expressed their own feelings of remorse, namely "hey, we should have said something when the doctors wouldn't let you sign." Some of their friends have asked them repeatedly why they didn't, and it is hard for them to come up with an answer that makes sense. However, those were the days when there were few TTYs, no relay services, no captioned TV, no universal acceptance of a Deaf culture, and so on. ASL had yet to be recognized as a bona fide language in its own right... and without that kind of power, there really weren't any good opportunities for me in the Deaf world. They would arise later, in due time. So for the time being, my parents went along with whatever the hearing world said was best for me.

Chapter 3

Granted, my family background is somewhat unusual compared to most deaf people. According to most sources, about ninety percent of deaf people have hearing parents. The ten percent of deaf people who do have deaf parents are often considered the lucky ones. While many deaf children of hearing parents usually fall behind in terms of linguistic development because they cannot hear the spoken language of their parents, deaf children of deaf parents experience no such communication gap. Their language, American Sign Language, is visual instead of aural, but a language nonetheless. This crucial access to language allows normal linguistic and cognitive development to take place, what with the many learning experiences that arise naturally amongst parents and children who can communicate effectively.

And then there are the social advantages, such as never being left out of conversations and enjoying all kinds of family outings. Deaf children of deaf parents usually have access to everything going on around them; there is no wondering what is being said, and none of the painful "nevermind, it wasn't important" brush-offs that are all too common with hearing relatives and friends who don't sign. In Deaf families the information is right there, in ASL, for Deaf children to enjoy and assimilate.

All in all, Deaf children of Deaf parents are considered lucky because:

- They have strong linguistic background, often very fluent in both ASL and written English.
- They live in a more sociably favorable home environment.

- They are also held in high esteem by the Deaf community in general, and tend to have strong leadership qualities that help them gain power and prestige. The skills they pick up while fully immersed in the Deaf world are often skills that they can carry over and utilize in the hearing world.

So, in my case, *what happened?* My family experience has been anything but what you'd expect from a deaf child of Deaf parents. People today still see me signing and assume I'm hearing, hard of hearing, or a "hearie-minded" deaf guy. Often, their jaws drop when they eventually find out I come from a Deaf family. And they scratch their heads even more when I try to explain the dynamics of my family background, which is no easy task. No matter what I say, the question always remains: how could a deaf child be surrounded by so much deafness in his family, and still not internalize it as part of his own identity? Very good question, and one that's still difficult to answer.

To many Deaf people, having Deaf parents is a badge of honor. Currently, I understand why this is so, and of course I'm proud of my folks. But while I was growing up, I never had an inkling that it was so special. First of all, hearing family members were acting on doctors' advice to fix, and in effect deny, my deafness. This convinced me that deafness was something to be ashamed of, not proud of.

Secondly, my mother's closest friends in the Deaf community also happened to have Deaf children, so I came to the conclusion that it was the norm for Deaf people to have Deaf kids. I never really appreciated how lucky I was to have Deaf parents who understood my struggles until I was college-age, when Deaf friends of mine made a big deal out of it.

And when people try to figure out how a deaf child of Deaf parents can go twenty-plus years with minimal use of sign language, they look at my family background for answers... and instead, they find more questions. Further adding to the confusion is the fact that there are plenty other Deaf people in my family besides just my mother and father. Whereas my mother is the only Deaf person on her side of the family, my father's side is predominantly Deaf.

Basically, it goes like this: my father's late parents, Cloyd Drolsbaugh and Marjorie (Margie) Schooley Drolsbaugh, were Deaf. Cloyd came from a hearing family, but Margie's family has a long history of deafness. There are several Deaf aunts, uncles and cousins from the Schooley family whom I've been in touch with from time to time. In fact, there would be an odd family reunion of sorts years later when I attended Gallaudet University: two distant cousins, Trina Schooley and Dan Warthling, were also enrolled at Gallaudet. None of us really knew each other until then. Imagine bumping into two people in a big university, getting a good conversation going, and then realizing "Oh, we're family." Weird, yes, but it gives you an idea of how large my father's family is.

So while my mother's hearing family was all close-knit and living in Philadelphia, my father's was spread out all over Pennsylvania. Many are in Scranton/Wilkes-Barre and Juniata County, most of whom I have yet to meet. My paternal grandparents, Margie and Cloyd, lived in Philadelphia for a considerable time, but moved back to Scranton when I was six or seven years old. Margie would again relocate to Philadelphia when I was about thirteen; by then, Cloyd had died and Margie wound up getting married again, to Michael Novak (also Deaf).

It must also be noted that my contact with the Deaf side of the family, due to geographic factors, ranged from

21

occasional to sporadic. We usually got together during Christmas, Easter, or someone's birthday. The Deaf family members I saw most frequently were my grandmother Margie (who we affectionately called Nana), my stepgrandfather Mike, and my Uncle Bob and Aunt Libby.

There are a variety of reasons why my exposure to Deaf family members didn't result in my becoming a native ASL signer. First of all, during the early years of my life, I was hearing or pretty close to hearing. I did not have an urgent need to pick up sign language. I could understand my parents' signing, but I hardly signed much myself. When I did sign, it was just some basic signs mixed up with "home signs," just enough to get the message through.

Also, not all of the Deaf people in my family are very fluent in ASL. Most of them have used local and home signs that were not prevalent in mainstream Deaf society. A number of them attended oral schools, where sign language was not permitted, so they themselves were late at picking up sign language and thus they were not native signers. Some of them were hearing or hard-of-hearing at an early age before going deaf later, such as my father and Uncle Bob (I followed this pattern myself). They often used a combination of signing and voice, depending on whom they were interacting with. Most of my recollections of family get-togethers evoke memories of a communication style closer to what is known as sim-com (simultaneous communication, utilizing both voice and sign). However, my mother and my Aunt Libby (both prelingually Deaf) have always used ASL, and I recall other family members signing more fluently while in Deaf clubs or other situations where most everyone else was Deaf.

Yet another reason is the fact that as I was seeing my father's Deaf family only occasionally, I saw my mother's hearing family all the time. When my hearing loss was discovered, they were devastated and went overboard trying to help me. As previously mentioned, they searched for professional advice that turned out to be anything but. They wound up following doctors' orders and discouraged me from signing, as well as asking my parents to refrain from signing with me. Perhaps they were able to exert their influence on me more than any other family members, simply because I saw them all the time.

Finally, perhaps most significantly, another explanation for my initially poor signing skills can be found by looking at who my peers were. Virtually all of them were hearing. The neighborhood kids I played with were hearing. My classmates were hearing. When my parents visited Uncle Bob and Aunt Libby, I played with their hearing daughters, Mary and Nora. Anyone who knows anything about sociology will tell you that we learn most from our peers, so I guess this explains best why I didn't sign so much at an early age. Monkey see, monkey do. All of my peers were using voice, so I did the same. Since I was postlingually deaf and still had enough residual hearing to be able to talk, I did. Being surrounded by hearing peers, to me, meant I had to be like them. I managed to do reasonably well most of the time, but later I would stumble.

However, despite the fact that I appeared to be more like a hearing person, it's not like I was completely shut off from the Deaf world. How could I be? After all, I was born into it. No matter how much I was under pressure to adapt to the hearing world, my parents were still a part of Deaf culture. Besides my Deaf family, I got to see other Deaf people when my parents took me with them to the local Deaf club. I saw many Deaf adults, but perhaps I was not Deaf enough myself to relate to them. I did, however, get a good taste of what the Deaf world was like.

Back in those days, TTYs had just gone on the market, and they were noisy, oversized machines that were no substitute for face-to-face conversation. Many Deaf people had yet to get a TTY, so they often went to the local Deaf club on a weekly or monthly basis. This resulted in a phenomenon that I call the infamous Deaf Chat Syndrome. It was not uncommon to stay until the wee hours of the morning, as each gathering was an opportunity to catch up on a month's worth of news. Likewise, when friends visited each other, the visits were often unannounced and would last for hours.

My mother would take me on such visits. Usually we visited her good friend, Carol. Often, I would watch my mother in amazement: *does she ever run out of things to say?* Apparently not! Although I enjoyed playing with her friend's children, by ten p.m. I'd had enough. And then the whining would start:

Can we go home now?

My mother would say yes, just a few more minutes. Those minutes would turn into hours, and my whining would grow louder.

I wanna go home... now!

At this juncture my mother would tell me to get my jacket... we were just about out of there. Alright! I would put on my jacket, my mother would head for the door, and... chat some more. I'd be tugging at her pants as she stood in the hallway, chatting up a storm.

For the umpteenth time, I would remind her it was time to go home. Ah-ha, she would move to the doorway... and yes, you guessed it, continue yakking. It seemed that each conversational tidbit took on a life of its own... heaven forbid somebody briefly mentioned something new on the way out, for a brand new conversation would spawn right on the spot. For example:

"Okay, I'll see you next week... don't forget to tell Laura I said hello..."

"Oh, sure, I saw Laura last week, she's going to the shore with Ted..."

"What? She's seeing Ted now? Last time I saw her... blah blah blah." Blah blah blah ad infinitum, ad nauseum.

All I can say about this experience is that I learned a great deal about the word patience, and that no conversation was over until my mother started the car and backed out of the driveway. I just chalked it up as something that went on in my mother's Deaf world. For as much as I made fun of her for her unlimited chat potential, I would eventually discover that it was hereditary; years later, I would succumb to Deaf Chat Syndrome myself, even writing an article about it that was titled *Help! I'm Signing and I Can't Shut Up!* Maybe, as an eight year old, I never knew it... but perhaps I was subconsciously taking notes and learning how to be culturally Deaf. I was always fascinated with my parent's Deaf friends, the Deaf clubs they went to, and their wholesome sense of humor. But as a youngster, somehow I was still on the outside looking in.

Once I began second grade at Houston School, it became more and more obvious that I wouldn't survive there. Class was considerably larger, about twenty or twenty-five children. There was more information to learn, information that simply went over my head. I remember taking spelling tests where the teacher would walk around the room reciting the words we needed to write down, and I routinely handed in a blank piece of paper. I felt terribly inadequate when I did so. There was no way, at *t*his age, that I could reason it was not my fault. Based on the actions of hearing family members, teachers and students, I perceived that I was some kind of defective freak. Deafness was bad, I was bad... I needed to be fixed.

Being "fixed" was no joy, believe me. My family kept sending me to doctors and audiologists, all the while reinforcing my mistaken belief that I was a freak of nature. My ears were tested so often, I learned by rote the entire wordsheet that audiologists read to you at varying frequencies:

"Say the word... *hot dog*."

"Say the word... *toothbrush*." This was worse than Chinese water torture. Say the word... nauseated.

Despite the way I felt in the audiologist booth, however, it is not my intention to attack the audiology profession. Audiologists are crucial for the purpose of assessment and placement. There is, however, a reasonable limit to how many times you can be tested and retested... my limit was exceeded to the point where even my ear, nose and throat doctor told my grandfather to get a grip and start accepting my hearing loss.

Furthermore, it didn't do me any good to be placed in an environment where I would repeatedly fail at something. There is no actual "pass-or-fail" as far as audiological tests are concerned, but no one took the time to explain that to me. They should have. Today, an increasing number of audiologists are fluent in sign language, and thus are able to explain to deaf children that hearing tests are merely evaluations which will help other people accommodate their needs. In my opinion, this ability to communicate with clients should be an absolute must. I say this because I felt like an insignificant guinea pig when I was tested. I was completely terrorized, felt like I was failing miserably, and also felt like I was letting my family down. I usually didn't mind the "raise your hand at the beep" routine, because that was relatively simple. If I heard a beep, I would raise my hand. If I didn't hear a beep, I didn't know if I missed something. When it came to the part where I had to repeat words and sentences the audiologist said (without being permitted to read her lips), that's when I began to feel like an incompetent fool.

Incompetent fool or not, I was fitted with two hearing aids which did nothing but make my life even more miserable. Hearing adults suddenly expected me to hear everything that was said, further intimidating me into believing I had to be like them. I began "nodding", saying yes to everything people said without having the slightest clue what they were talking about. Yes, their voices were certainly louder when I wore the hearing aids, but my ability to understand their speech showed no significant improvement. The only advantage of having hearing aids, for me, was that I could actually hear the toilet flush from the next room. This must have been culturally significant... it was around that time that the first toilet was flushed on national television, when Archie Bunker did the honors on *All in the Family*. I am eternally grateful to my family and medical professionals for making it possible for me to share this special moment.

In school, though, there was nothing special about wearing hearing aids. I was made fun of and ridiculed. Second grade was the only time in my life where I routinely got into fights and received report cards that said my behavior left much to be desired. It was obvious that there was no way I could keep this up.

At this juncture, my grandparents went out and did the best favor they ever could have done for me at the time. They did their homework, checked out a number of possibilities, and enrolled me at Plymouth Meeting Friends School. A small private school outside of Philadelphia, PMFS offered a cozy learning environment that would be a welcome change from the crowded classes at Houston School. Also, I didn't know it while I was there, but PMFS' Quaker background and philosophy would later have a tremendous impact on my personal growth.

Entering the third grade at PMFS, of course I was apprehensive. Of course I thought I was going to be the laughingstock of the class, and of course I had to be on my guard at all times. Apparently, I was wrong. What with its small student population, there were only about eight kids in each class. In addition to that, each class had a teacher aide, meaning the student-teacher ratio was a comfortable 4:1. It was very clear from the start that I would get much-needed individual attention, and I did. Anytime I missed instructions (and that was quite often) the teacher aide would zoom to the rescue, fill me in on the details, and I would be right up with the rest of the class in schoolwork.

While it was clear I would be in good hands academically, I was concerned about my social life. Memories of the taunts and fights I put up with at Houston School were still fresh in my mind. However, my third grade teacher, Mrs. Paul, had gone out of her way to make me feel welcome at PMFS. She had previously explained to her class that there would be a hard-of-hearing boy joining them, and she encouraged them to ask questions so that they knew what to expect. She encouraged them to speak clearly so that I could read their lips and feel like I was part of the class. I was certainly grateful when I noticed that I was accepted warmly. There was some curiosity about what I was like and how my hearing aids worked, but no one made fun of me. Mrs. Paul did an excellent job of helping us all go through this transition.

Old habits die hard, though, so I was still on my guard for a while before I completely settled down at PMFS. I figured it was only a matter of time before some moron would poke fun at me and I'd have to defend myself. Most of the kids quickly got along with me, but I was just waiting for that one idiot who always has to screw everything up. There was one boy, Quinn, who seemed to be making fun of me. Actually, he was making fun of everyone and everything. He was one of those fun types who was always laughing and cracking jokes. Nonetheless, I eyed him suspiciously and didn't like him. Anytime he laughed, I figured it had to be something about me.

Finally, on one cold winter day, we were all outside playing snow football. We were having a blast tackling each other in the snow and sliding all over the place. Suddenly, when I had the ball, Quinn delivered a good hit and knocked the wind out of me. Normally I would have been a good sport, but this particular hit knocked a hearing aid right off my ear. It was a quick and sudden reminder to everyone that I was *different.*

To make matters worse, the battery had come loose and fell out. It was lost somewhere on a vast field, hidden under six inches of snow. I made a fuss over the battery, but actually it was just my pride that was hurt. When we returned to class, Mrs. Paul heard about what happened from one of the students. She approached me and asked me about the battery. A number of students were standing around her, showing as much concern as she was.

"Do you have another battery at home?"

"Nope," I said, feeling sorry for myself. Quinn, the guy who I knew would make fun of me, walked up.

"How much does it cost for a new one?"

"About one hundred dollars," I whined. One hundred dollars, my ass. You can replace a hearing aid battery as quickly and as cheaply as a regular wristwatch battery. But I was the class freak (or so I thought), so I figured if the equipment I had was incredibly expensive, then I must be incredibly *important*. Right after I gave this incredibly exaggerated value of the hearing aid battery, some of the students volunteered to go out and look for it.

And look for it they did, on a football field covered with six inches of snow. Given that a hearing aid battery is less than half the size of a marble, this would be much harder than looking for the proverbial needle in a haystack. It should have been touching enough that they were so considerate that they tried looking for it. But they went way beyond that. They searched high and low and *found it*. They actually found the damn thing. It was none other than Quinn who rushed in, smiling proudly, handing me my one hundred-dollar battery. The lesson I learned in friendship that day was worth a million bucks.

After the hearing aid incident, I became more comfortable at PMFS, and I had no problem getting along with others. I related quite well with my classmates, who were as accommodating as the staff. My best friend, Norman, would call me up on the phone during evenings and weekends, patiently repeating words or even spelling them until I understood what he was saying. In class, other students often took the burden off of the teacher aide by repeating instructions or assignments that I didn't understand. With this kind of support, I no longer felt ashamed or embarrassed of my deafness, the way I was beginning to feel after my frustrations at Houston School.

I began to feel I was fitting in so well, that I was practically as hearing as everyone else. When it was suggested that I take up speech therapy, I gladly consented, because I viewed it as something that would make me even more hearing. It would, my grandparents assured me, help me speak the same way as everyone else. I figured why not... I was so encouraged by the way I was fitting in at PMFS, that I perceived speech therapy as icing on the cake... I was finally going to look, act and *talk* like a hearing person.

My speech teacher, Mrs. Wells, turned out to be a funny, creative person who knew how to make what was really a dreary activity a whole lot more fun than it actually was. She did not exhibit the "we need to fix you" sense of urgency that I had perceived from other professionals. If I pronounced a word wrong, she would make a funny face, get me laughing, and encourage me to get it right. When I did get a tough word right, I would gleefully repeat it until she would scream,

"Aaarrggghh!!! No more! I'm sick of that word!" The more success I had, the more she let me drive her up the wall. I would come home and brag to my family that I was so good at what I did, I was driving her nuts. I was on the road to Hearing Person, and very proud of it.

After about two years of speech therapy, however, I had a rather humbling wake-up call. My mother had introduced me to a hearing acquaintance of hers, with whom I proudly held a brief conversation. Although my mother's friend knew sign language, I kept my hands to myself and used my speech. I managed to go through the customary "how are you", "nice to meet you", and "hope to see you again sometime"... all without having to ask this woman to repeat anything she said. On top of that, I didn't even stutter once, smoothly going through those damned R's that used to give me a hard time. I was very proud of myself and beamed accordingly. My pride, however, soon took a nose-dive. As my mother's friend walked to her car, I caught her signed conversation with my mom:

"Is your son hard of hearing?"

"Yes," my mom responded. "His hearing is slowly going down... same as his father and Uncle Bob... it's hereditary."

"Yes, I could tell by his voice..."

My heart sank. I would continue to do my best to be as hearing as possible for the next several years, but this was a real smack in the face. Reality was a bummer. People would continue pushing for me to be as hearing as possible, and I would still do my best to comply. Deep down, however, I knew I would always be different.

Fortunately, if there was ever a good place to be different and still be accepted anyway, PMFS was it. As for all of my issues relating to deafness which I am bringing up in this book, there is nothing further to say regarding my years there. I was part of one big family, and I loved every minute of it. I don't recall sticking out like a sore thumb... grades three through six were the wonder years for me. It must have been the calm before the storm. We'll get to that storm later... the adolescent hell also known as high school.

Chapter 4

School was not the only place where I would struggle with deafness. There were other aspects of life to deal with, such as religion. My experience with religion has been just as complicated as anything I went through in school, perhaps even more so. School is where we learn the ABC's and the basics of life with all of our peers; religion is more of an internal struggle, a path we ultimately choose to pursue alone.

My path towards spiritual growth has taken countless detours, but every venture off the beaten path has been a blessing in disguise. For the most part, my search for the meaning of life has taken me through Judaism, Christianity, Quakerism and a deep fascination with Eastern Philosophy. I never really did fit into any one particular traditional religion, though. Some may argue that this is a negative consequence of deafness, but I choose to look at it differently. The positive side to all of this is that by never actually fitting into just one, I could appreciate all. It took a long time, a lot of soul-searching, but eventually I would find my own personal niche.

The first step, for me, was Judaism. Although my mother and father did not always observe any religious holidays at home, my mother came from a Jewish family that played by all the rules. In fact, my grandfather himself was an ordained rabbi. A pretty good one, I must add. My character has been greatly shaped by the lessons I learned through him. Unfortunately, my hearing loss prevented me from completely assimilating the religion he loved so much, but nonetheless it still had a major impact on me. I might have had all of the rules of organized religion fly over my head, but at least I managed to pick up the essence of them. For example, one day I was riding on the highway with my grandfather when all of a sudden, some moron zoomed up a ramp, ignored a yield sign, and began to cut us off. All my grandfather did was apply the brakes, let the maniac cut through, then go about his driving as if nothing happened.

"Grandpop?" I asked. "Why did you let him do that?" Grandpop just smiled.

"I don't want to prove, with a broken arm, that I had the right of way".

That lesson in humility and egolessness stuck with me for a long time. In this day and age of people flipping each other the finger and even shooting semi-automatic weapons on the highways, we could sure use more people like good old Grandpop.

For the most part, my involvement with religion was pretty much learning by doing, anecdotal lessons like the one with my grandfather. I never really learned any specific religious dogma or the meaning behind it; I never fully understood why my grandparents would light a candle at certain times on certain days. However, as they went about their daily lives in accordance with their religious philosophy, I was able to emulate general behaviors such as being compassionate and caring amongst one another. Like I said, I pretty much skipped the dogma and went straight to the essence. Other than that, I generally enjoyed accompanying my grandmother and grandfather to the synagogue, even if I never really understood what was going on. I enjoyed the half-hour drive, playing brainteaser games with Grandmom the whole way ("I'm thinking of a number...") and then proudly watching Grandpop preach his stuff at the synagogue. *Yessiree, that's my grandfather up there. What the hell he's saying, I have no idea, but that's my grandfather up there.* That sort of thing. I was proud of him.

As I got older, though, I began having problems with religion. The first problem, simply put, was that everyone started expecting me to understand what was going on around me. While religion to my mother and father simply meant showing up at whatever family events were going on, my grandparents took a more vested interest in my religious development. When I was about ten or eleven, I had made so much progress as a student at Plymouth Meeting Friends School that they expected me to likewise learn quickly in the synagogue. I was briefly enrolled in a Sunday Hebrew School, but I completely bombed. It was like Houston School all over again. I had no idea of what was going on around me, there were too many kids, and I was being made fun of. There was no way I could learn Hebrew in there. I had enough trouble understanding people speaking plain English, so what could they have possibly been expecting from me?

Did I ever speak up? Of course not. Due to the earlier reactions to my deafness by my hearing family and various professionals (the aforementioned Diagnostic Crisis), it was already ingrained in my head that deafness was bad. In a way, I was being behaviorally conditioned. Anytime I was able to understand hearing people or speak clearly, I was praised; anytime I had difficulty understanding others or mispronounced words, all of the hearing people in my life reacted with grave concern. Deafness was bad, period, so there was no way I could defend myself as being treated unfairly because I was deaf. If I couldn't understand all those people in Hebrew School, it was my fault.

To make matters even worse, Hebrew School wasn't the half of it. I bombed so badly, that my grandfather mercifully bailed me out and decided he would teach me himself. He was determined that by age thirteen, I would know enough to have a Bar Mitzvah (to his delight, I eventually did). And so he began to teach me. He did quite well, but it was not always a smooth ride. Yes, Grandpop was very patient and accommodating as he taught me what I needed to know. What I got from him in these individual sessions, I had no problem assimilating. Everything else, such as whatever went on in the synagogue or during family celebrations, went over my head as always. No one really understood this except for my own parents, who weren't really involved anyway. For whatever reason, perhaps denial or just plain ignorance, everyone else in the family had unrealistic expectations for me. As far as they were concerned, I was a hearing Jewish boy. A common scenario: a day or so before any significant Jewish holiday, a hearing family member would smile at me and say,

"Mark, do you know what tomorrow is?" My palms would already be sweaty, for I knew what was coming.

"Uhhhhh," I would stammer meekly.

"Oh, come on, you know what it is! Tomorrow is Purim. Do you know what Purim is all about?" I would be completely cornered here. At best, I would take a wild guess, but most of the time I'd just shrug helplessly. This would be enough to set off a nuclear reaction. Disaster was imminent, I knew it was coming. First, it would be a gasp of shock, followed by heads shaking disapprovingly. Then came the barrage:

"Mark! You should know what it is! It's your heritage! You should know!"

Yeah, right. I should know. For the life of me, I wish I could turn back the clock and shoot back:

"How the hell should I know? You guys chatter incessantly and expect me to just soak it up like a sponge? Hasn't anyone told you I'm deaf? If it's so damn important, why don't you learn sign language and then tell me what it is I need to know? *You* should know what it's like to be

deaf. Don't be giving me any of this *you should know...*"
Of course, I never spoke up. Deafness is bad. Be hearing.
Good boy, be hearing.

Obviously, my hearing family could frustrate me
sometimes. Yet if they gave me a hard time about my
deafness, they had no idea they were doing so. At least in
other ways, they gave me plenty of love and attention. So
if I had any bad experiences with my family, they were
always related to deafness or religion. Those are just two
aspects of my world. In many others, my family was loving
and supportive. We all play a number of roles in life...
some of mine, for example, are son, grandson, husband,
father, student, athlete, and deaf person. Most of my roles
have been supported one hundred percent by my family.
For my role as deaf person, they just weren't sure what to
do. And neither was I, seeing how I meekly tiptoed around
the subject whenever it arose.

Despite my early frustrations with Judaism, despite
several occasions where I had no idea what was going
on... it needs to be mentioned that somehow, I nonetheless
was greatly influenced by Jewish philosophy. My
grandfather's wisdom and my grandmother's strong
family values are parts of my background that I will always
hold on to. It gave me a foundation from which I could
build on. There would more religions that I would become
involved with, all of them shaping in some way my
philosophy of life, but I will never forget where I came
from.

School and religion, no doubt, were roller coaster
rides consisting of both enjoyment and frustration. While
we all, in our own unique ways, go through various
growing pains, we also need some sort of outlet to make
life more bearable for us. For me, this outlet was baseball.
Away from the pressures of school, away from the high
expectations of my family, I just threw myself into baseball

full-time each summer. I was fortunate to grow up in a time when my role models, the Philadelphia Phillies of the 70's and 80's, played together as a team year in and year out. Back then, I could count on seeing my favorite players every year. These days, players demand to be traded or opt for free agency because they're insulted that their multi-million dollar contract is not the highest salary in the league. Poor babies. At least I'm grateful that in my time, I got to see guys who played hard, day in and day out, and loved the game. I was certainly able to emulate them.

And emulate them I did, playing baseball from twelve noon until whenever the sun went down. In my neighborhood, this meant whiffle ball, stickball, sandlot hardball and eventually organized Little League. Looking back, I realize that during those sandlot days, I was immortal. I was too young to be aware of all of the hard struggles that would be waiting for me a few years later. I was too young to understand that someday, we all grow old and eventually die. I was too young to worry about it. This must be what all the great masters have meant when they preached the virtues of living in the now, the present moment. By playing ball all day, oblivious to all the hassles of the adult world, we had a taste of nirvana. It's sad that in today's era, many kids are exposed too soon to the horrors of drugs and violence. They grow up too fast, and miss out on the carefree childhood experiences that are greatly rewarding. I was lucky to live in a time and place where I could just let go and taste life.

My neighborhood was the Mt. Airy section of Philadelphia, pretty much a racially mixed area. There were Italian families on one side of the neighborhood, and African-American families just up the street. I don't know if it was because of the proximity or some complicated social dynamics, but I wound up being closest to an African-American family even though at first glance it would appear we didn't have much in common. My best friend's name was Sekou, and though we were culturally different, we shared an immense love for baseball. Sekou had no problem with me being deaf; I had no problem with him being black. What was the big deal? We had a lot of fun playing baseball, and that was that.

To other people though, it might have been a big deal, although for a while I wasn't aware of it. After playing countless hours of baseball in my backyard, my friends and I eventually became so good at it that we would play games against other sandlot teams and routinely beat them. Finally, one day, while driving with my mom through the suburbs, I saw a Little League game being played. It was on a beautiful grass field, complete with scoreboards and dugouts. I told my mom that it would be perfect for Sekou and me, because I knew we could play at that level. She shook her head sadly and began to explain something I could not understand. We were only five or six years removed from the Civil Rights movement and Martin Luther King Jr.'s tragic assassination, and there were still some neighborhoods where blacks were just not welcome. While Sekou was legally entitled to play on any Little League team he wanted, there were many who would make his life miserable. I just could not grasp this. Here was one of few people who unconditionally accepted me for who I was, and his *skin color* was a big deal? This was stupid. As far as I was concerned, Little League could wait.

Meanwhile, we continue to play sandlot ball all summer, and Sekou's family taught me something which I would not comprehend until much later... sort of a

39

retrospective lesson in life. While I was struggling with my deafness, trying to act like a hearing boy and dealing with the embarrassment of being made fun of, Sekou's family was holding their heads up high. They were black, they were proud, and they didn't give a damn that some prejudiced morons in the world couldn't accept them for who they were. They often dressed in beautiful African clothes, and their house was loaded with African paintings, sculptures and artifacts. Sekou's mother and father always welcomed me into their house, and they proudly shared their world with me.

One time, Sekou's father took me along with the kids to their favorite barbershop. I was in a room full of about twenty other people, none of them white. I was the only one. I was about ten or eleven at the time, and it was a strange feeling, sticking out the way that I did. I believe that Sekou's father wanted to give me an idea of what it feels like to be a racial minority. For the first time, I really understood how Sekou must have felt whenever we ventured into a predominantly white neighborhood for a sandlot game. I realize now that there is no better lesson to learn than empathy and compassion for another's perspective, and to be able to walk a mile in someone else's moccasins.

Looking back, I also realize that I could have done a better job of learning another lesson: how to be proud of your own culture. If my Deaf parents and I had half the pride in being Deaf that Sekou's family had in being black, then most of our problems would have been eliminated right there. Of course, I learned this lesson slowly, given my tendency to do things the hard way.

Eventually, Sekou's family packed their bags and moved downtown, closer to the church they routinely attended. I would make other friends, both black and white, and we all kept playing baseball. Before Sekou moved, though, there was one game we played that I'll never forget. We were challenged to a sandlot game in another part of the neighborhood, in the backyard of Grace Church. The challenge was issued by an all-white baseball team a few blocks away, and they told us to make sure we had at least nine players; this was going to be real *baseball*. So we looked around and found as many neighborhood kids as we could. We managed to round up about twelve people, but only five or six of us were genuinely experienced baseball players. To fill out the remaining positions for the nine-on-nine game, we had to get some guys who were acquaintances of ours but never really played baseball that much.

When we arrived at the sandlot field, we noticed that the other team was *big*. Many of them I had never seen before in the neighborhood... my feeling at first was that this was not about baseball, but more likely a black vs. white thing. Someone on the other team made a disparaging remark about me being the only white guy on my team... the first pitch had yet to be thrown, and already racism was rearing its ugly head.

Once the game started, though, something wonderful was happening. We all began having a lot of fun... we forgot about color, and focused on baseball. Not that it helped my team, though. Our opponents were really good, and they were giving us quite a drubbing. By the ninth inning, we were down, 13-0, although we were having a lot more fun than the score would have indicated.

With two outs in the top of the ninth, I stepped up to the plate. I ripped a hard line drive down rightfield and pulled into second base with a double. The next batter was Teddy, one of those extra players we pulled out of nowhere. I don't know who he was, but he ripped the stuffing out of the next pitch for a solid base hit, bringing me home with our only run of the game. As I crossed the plate, the team mobbed me like we had just won the seventh game of the World Series, screaming and hugging. It was the warmest moment I've ever experienced in all sports, including championships I would later be a part of in high school and organized baseball. We all learned something about brotherhood that day... both teams, black and white.

Chapter 5

As the elementary school years drew to a close, it was time to start looking for a good high school. During my final year at Plymouth Meeting Friends School (which runs from kindergarten to grade six), my grandparents continued to ensure that I would get a quality education. They heard that Germantown Friends School was one of the best schools in Philadelphia, and they looked into the possibility of enrolling me there. Being another Friends' school, GFS would provide a continuation of the teaching style and Quaker philosophy I had grown accustomed to at PMFS. Of course, bottom line, this was a fantastic high school we were looking into. This was practically Harvard High School, seeing how many GFS graduates have gone on to greater success in Ivy League colleges.

It was soon decided that GFS would be my next stop on the academic ladder. Along with five other PMFS classmates, I took an entry exam at GFS, which was to determine if we had what it takes to survive the challenging curriculum. A few weeks later, we whooped it up in celebration when we found out we'd all been accepted.

Whoa, not so fast. The other five were definitely in. As far as the entry exam indicated, so was I... but a few things needed to be cleared up first. The faculty at GFS had heard about my promising academic potential, but they also knew about my deafness. This was not the cute, cozy environment of PMFS; this was a relatively large school with nine hundred students. It needed to be assessed whether or not I could survive in what could be, for me, a potentially hostile environment. A one-day visit was scheduled, so that I could get a taste of life at GFS.

This one-day visit is granted to all incoming GFS students, so that they know what to expect when they enroll... for me, however, this visit was going to be the final say in whether or not I would be accepted as a student there. Not only would I get to see what life at GFS was like, but also the faculty would be evaluating my ability to get along in a large hearing school. When I arrived at GFS one day for my visit, I knew damn well what the stakes were. My grandfather had explained, loud and clear, what the real purpose of this visit was. I knew he was really rooting for me to get in, and I didn't want to let him down.

To GFS' credit, they didn't beat around the bush with me. I was escorted to a Mr. Emerson's office, and he got right down to the bottom line: he was happy to see me there, but also wanted to see how my deafness would affect me in the classroom. I would attend a number of classes and then return at the end of the day to discuss how it went. My escort for the day was then ushered in. I smiled when I realized it was an old neighborhood friend of mine, a boy named Ian. Whether this was prearranged or just plain dumb luck, I don't know. Either way, I was certainly grateful to have him showing me around. Of course we hit it off well, because we'd grown up next door from each other... and this certainly helped my case, as the teachers took note that I was interacting quite well with him and his friends.

To be honest, though, ninety-five percent of the time that day I had no idea what was going on. It was a big school, and it was somewhat intimidating. If it weren't for Ian, I would have run out of there completely terrorized. I could see very well that this could wind up being the high school version of Houston School: a cold, crowded environment packed with people who would ridicule me and my deafness. Classes were a blur; I didn't understand one word of what was being said around me. I just smiled when other people smiled, chuckled when other people chuckled, and tried my best to look like I fit in. I didn't want to let my grandfather down, and I didn't plan to. I was getting into this school, even if I had to put on an Oscar performance to do it.

Finally, at the end of the day, I returned to Mr. Emerson's office. Conversing with him was no problem, because I was pretty much okay in one-to-one conversations. It was the groups, particularly classrooms, which had me lost in space. Mr. Emerson began by asking me how my day was, and I replied that it was just fine and dandy. He probed a bit more, asking how I felt my deafness affected me. I assured him that I was on top of everything, understood pretty much of what was going on around me, and had enjoyed my visit. Then I gave him the same baloney my grandfather had told everyone: with a hearing aid, I'm practically the same as any other normal kid. That was it; I was in. I was full of bull, but I was in. *The nominee for best actor is...*

Settling in at GFS was not going to be easy. I knew it, my family knew it. My grandfather, though, had an experience that would enable him to give me a little pep talk. It turned out that while he was at a local swim club, he met a deaf adult, Dr. Cash, who happened to be a prominent surgeon. I'd heard of him before, and was surprised to find out that he had a long heart-to-heart talk with my grandfather. It was the first time Grandpop had met such a successful deaf adult, and he took advantage of the opportunity to discuss a number of issues related to deafness.

Shortly before I was to begin the seventh grade at GFS, my grandfather decided to share with me one of the topics he brought up with Dr. Cash. He pulled me aside and said,

"Mark, you remember Dr. Cash, the surgeon? You know, he has a hearing problem just like yours, and he's a doctor. Well, I was talking to him about you going to GFS, and he doesn't think you're gonna make it."

Oh great, I thought. Nice way to boost my confidence.

"Incidentally," my grandfather continued, "Dr. Cash said that no deaf person ever has, nor ever will graduate from GFS. I think you can prove him wrong."

Now I was getting psyched…I guess some kind of pride inside me clicked. Yes, I knew Dr. Cash was only being realistic; he knew firsthand that GFS was a tough school for anyone. There were enough academic challenges there as it was; throw in a progressively worsening hearing loss, and that might have been one challenge too many. Nonetheless, I was determined to show I had what it takes. I knew it was going to be a formidable task, but I was going to make it.

But as determined as I was to succeed at GFS, it immediately became a difficult transition. At PMFS, everyone knew me and I was also one of the best athletes in the whole school. At GFS, I was just a face in the crowd, and a mediocre athlete among the many students. I was lost in the classroom, and relegated to the "B" squad on the soccer team. These are normal frustrations experienced by anyone who moves to a bigger school… but for me they were magnified, as my deafness made it so much harder to adapt. It was hard to make new friends, and it was hard to believe I'd ever be comfortable there because I understood so little of what was going on. It was a pain in the neck trying to read everyone's lips; it was a pain in the neck being reminded by homeroom teachers to wear my hearing aids and sit up front, as if it would help (it didn't). Each class was a considerable amount of stress for me; I would worry that the teacher would call on me, and that I'd make a fool out of myself because I was so lost.

Really, I myself was part of the problem... I felt pressure to fit in with hearing students, and I had tried my best to always look like I knew what was going on. My daily routine consisted of trying my damnedest to understand what was happening in class, yet at the same time trying to maintain an air of nonchalance so that it looked like I was comfortably fitting in. Nonetheless, a teacher would often approach me at the end of class to make sure I had been following everything alright. I would quickly brush off the teacher with false assurances that all was fine and dandy. A common scenario:

"Yes, Ms. Wilson, I'm doing fine, no problem."

(brief pause as the teacher leaves the classroom)

"Psssst! Hey Brian... what did she say the homework was?"

This was the essence of my seventh and eight grade education: bluff my way through class, run up to a student I knew I could depend on, and ask him what the homework was. With that information, I could go home or to the library, where I could read more and brush up on all of the information I had missed in class. In some ways, it wouldn't be off base to say that in my early years at GFS, I was self-educated.

Fortunately, it wasn't that all bad. I did have a considerable amount of support from some very special individuals, including a few students. One of them, Dean, was in my Latin class. He knew me a little bit through a summer baseball league, although we weren't on the same team. He knew me well enough, however, to know that I was bluffing my way through Latin.

47

Often, there were times I just couldn't understand what the teacher was asking me, and my face would turn red with embarrassment and frustration. Rather than risk further ridicule, I would be content with saying "I don't know" and letting someone else answer the question. Dean was on to me, though. Sometimes I would respond with an "I don't know" to a ridiculously easy question, and Dean wouldn't let me get away with it. Imagine, for example, a substitute teacher coming in and asking me what my name was.

"Duh, I don't know."

Dean would jump in and help me save face. He would tap me on the shoulder, smile, and repeat the question slowly for me. His mannerisms made it clear that it was okay if I didn't understand what was going on; few people gave me this type of reinforcement. It was much appreciated.

As for the faculty, they were demanding, but they were also caring. They would challenge you in the classroom, making you think until your brains burst out of your ears. I knew I was in a really good school, because the teachers were never satisfied with concrete answers. If you wrote correctly on a term paper or in an exam about *what* happened, you would get credit for it of course, but there would be red ink comments everywhere on the paper. The teachers also wanted to know *why* it happened, what the dynamics were, and how things might have been different if... you get the idea. This was a school where you learned how to think outside the box. The teachers not only wanted the answers, they wanted us to come up with more questions.

In addition, they always took the time for private conferences with their students (incidentally, I had plenty) to be sure we were coming along okay and if anything could further be done to facilitate our development. So if I give the impression at times that I was unhappy at GFS, it had nothing to do with their program; I believe in my heart that GFS is the best high school anywhere. It's just that as the only deaf student, I was often like a fish out of water.

By the end of my first year at GFS, I would be rescued from academic hell by my beloved sport, baseball. Thanks to baseball, the year ended on a very positive note. I was a key part of the seventh grade baseball team, and was finally having fun again. I may have stunk up the soccer field and the basketball court, making only the "B" teams on both, but baseball was my turn to shine. We had a great team, and through baseball I made some more friends. Playing ball is a universal language for kids, it doesn't matter if you're deaf or Hindu or whatever. Fun is a language we all understand.

Around that time, however, there were some changes at home. My mother had accepted a new job at none other than the Pennsylvania School for the Deaf; she was working part time some evenings as a dorm counselor. This was a big change not just for her, but for me. Occasionally, there were times when my mom took me along with her to work. It was unbelievable. It was a totally, totally different world.

I have no idea of how I can adequately describe what it felt like the first time I walked into a whole school full of deaf children. It was an awakening, a rebirth of sorts, and all sorts of shackles broke free. I can only attempt to describe how I felt. Mere words can't express it adequately enough, but they'll have to do:

Imagine that you were born in some small Atlantis at the bottom of the sea, and the only life you knew was to live in some glass bubble underwater. You could watch all the fish swim and play, but you weren't really a participant in that life; you were nothing more than an observer to most of the things that happened around you. With the help of technology, though, you could put on scuba gear and swim with the fish. However, the gear was heavy and uncomfortable, and as much as it helped you interact with the fish, you never were able to swim like them. You were different, and you knew it.

Suddenly, one day, you decided to keep swimming upwards. Your friends, the fish, advised against it.

"Silly boy," they said. "Everyone knows it's a liquid world. You have nothing to gain by going up to the surface. Air is too thin, land is too hard. It's a liquid world."

You've heard that argument before, and you've always listened to it. This time, however, you felt that *it was time.* Time to find out who you really were, and everything you were all about. You swam all the way to the surface, and wonder of wonders, you found that there were thousands of people like you! You swam to the shore, and once you set your foot on land, you realized you didn't need all of that heavy scuba apparatus. You could run with the legs you were born with, and you could breathe freely in the natural air you were meant to breathe in. You could hold effortless conversations and have deep, meaningful relations with others. Freedom at last!

I can just see one of my old hearing classmates reading the above analogy and saying, "so what am I, a flounder?" No offense to my old classmates, but I genuinely felt a sense of freedom and involvement at PSD that I had never experienced anywhere else. When I met the other students in the PSD dorm for the first time, I felt a lightness, a jubilation that never existed before. No straining to read lips. No struggling to keep up with conversations going on between two or more people. No pressure to try to pass off as a hearing person. We were equals, and I was learning the value of true, meaningful interaction.

Everywhere I went, I could understand clearly what was being said, as everyone in PSD was signing. Although I had been discouraged from signing in my earlier years, I had picked up enough at home watching my mom and dad sign to each other. Even though I wasn't a completely fluent signer myself, I knew enough to be able to interact with the Deaf students at PSD. We played games, watched captioned movies, and had all kinds of fun. I never had to worry about fitting in or about catching up on missed information. The burden of trying to be something I'm not was temporarily lifted. Sign language was making my life bearable again.

Even my grandparents, who originally cooperated with doctors' assessment that I should not sign (on the erroneous premise that it was bad for my speech), took note that it was not the horrendous evil that it was made out to be. When my mother became more involved in the Deaf community through PSD, the changes in her self-esteem and demeanor were so positive, that for a short time my grandparents actually enrolled in sign language classes themselves.

One evening in the spring of 1978, PSD held a Springfest event, complete with carnival rides, games, fireworks, and a concert featuring songs performed in sign language. It was the most fun I had ever had in my neighborhood... Deaf and hearing alike were having the greatest time. My mind was made up then and there: soon, I would confront my parents.

When school was out and I felt the time was right, I approached my mom one evening and asked if I could be transferred to PSD. It wasn't fair to me that I had to be so isolated at GFS; it was no fun being the only deaf student. Except for the spring, when I had baseball games to look forward to, I never really enjoyed going to school in the morning. I dreaded classroom discussion, I dreaded embarrassing myself while misunderstanding teachers' questions or assignments, and heck, I was bombing with the girls. While some girls were nice enough to make polite conversation, none of them really wanted to get to know me on a deeper level. To be popular, they had to go out with the cool people, not disabled geeks like me. Lots of other guys had dates; I didn't.

At PSD, on the other hand, girls actually *liked* me. They talked to me freely about anything, and I even had a brief puppy-love thing going with one of them when I was fourteen. At GFS, I just wasn't getting any action. For a young, horny teenager, that's plenty of reason to transfer out of school.

Unfortunately, this horny teenager would have to wait. My mother and father gave me an emphatic NO. I was not going to transfer to PSD. My mother had actually given it some thought and looked into it, and made a grim discovery that she was not sure how to explain. The fact was, going into the eighth grade at GFS, I had already academically surpassed virtually all of the PSD seniors. English, math, science, you name it, I'd already done it. At PSD, I would have been taking an academic step backwards. At GFS, there were more mountains to climb. As my mother explained this, tears welled in my eyes.

"But mom, they're my *friends...*" My mother could only shake her head sadly. When my father heard how I felt about the whole thing, he tried to console me by sharing his own experience. When he was younger, he also had much potential, but he went to a deaf school. It did nothing for him. He began to explain a complicated social phenomenon I would not really understand until much later.

Since my father came from a Deaf family in Scranton, Pennsylvania, he was able to grow up in an environment where he had access to communication. Developmentally, he was on par with other hearing children. The only difference between deaf children of deaf families and hearing children of hearing families is mode of communication; one signs, the other speaks. As many parents will attest, a favorite word of young toddlers is "Why." Why does it get dark at night, why do I have to take a bath, why is the goldfish floating upside down, why do Aunt Emma's teeth fall out, why am I deaf. Why, why, why.

Whether amusing or a pain in the neck, we owe it to our children to answer as many of their whys as possible. When we do, the child is able to internalize crucial information, and overall development in terms of thought processing and general knowledge is facilitated.

Unfortunately, such favorable environments of communication do not exist for most deaf kids. Ninety percent of deaf children have hearing parents, and there is a communication gap. Often, hearing parents do not know sign language. The deaf child has to read lips, and reading lips is difficult; only about thirty-five percent of the spoken language can be lip-read (most sounds are formed in the back of the mouth). Imagine trying to answer all of your kid's "why" questions in such a manner that he or she can only understand thirty-five percent of what you're saying. Many parents try their best, only to give up in frustration. I've seen it happen many times, and it ticks me off. Instead of explaining various facts of life, many parents wave off the questions, say a "nevermind" which makes the kid feel he or she is not important, or they just say "no, don't do that" without explaining why it's not a good idea to set the cat on fire. No genuine communication, nothing learned. Just "don't do that."

Seeing how most deaf children come from hearing families that do not sign, they start their school years having to play catch-up. My father explained that when he moved to Philadelphia as a teenager, he attended two deaf schools, PSD and the Martin School. Not only did he have to pass time in classes where he was way ahead of everyone academically, but he also had to put up with the then-enforced oral philosophy of both schools. Sign language was forbidden, for the same reason doctors told my grandparents not to let me use it. It was believed that in order to be successful, all deaf people must speak. This philosophy has thrown a monkey wrench in the academic careers of countless deaf students. Many deaf children have gone through school learning nothing because they were being trained to be something they simply weren't.

If you had a choice, would you rather that your kid spent six years learning how to successfully pronounce the word "ball," or would you rather that those six years were spent signing clearly to him the concepts of modern science, literature and mathematics? This is a no-brainer, right? Guess again. Believe it or not, this argument is still hotly debated. Oralism has worked for some deaf children, and it has ruined the lives of others. It's a very controversial topic.

At PSD, however, the administration and the Deaf community eventually realized that the oral approach had resulted in more frustration than success. It was getting out of control. My father pointed out how one of his teachers used to hit him on the hands with a ruler whenever he signed... and one day, in total frustration, she actually began smacking him on the ears, hollering "you can hear! you can hear!"

My dad also told me about his friend Ted, who could never learn how to speak no matter how hard he tried. He would put in a good effort, but always to no avail. My father thought it was absolutely disgusting how the teachers would gush "oh, that's *wondderrrrfulllllll*" whenever Ted managed to emit a guttural sound that bore no resemblance to any spoken word whatsoever. At times like these, my dad confessed that he often wondered why they couldn't simply hold a class in sign language, so they could move on and cover material at a much faster rate. They were wasting time trying to pronounce "George Washington", without getting to whatever it was this Mr. Washington did that was so important.

Regardless, speech was a high priority, and my dad watched with curious amusement as the teachers picked on poor Ted. Finally, one of the teachers pushed Ted too far. Completely exasperated, Ted cut loose with the one word he could pronounce correctly:

"Fuck!"

My dad recalled how he had to do his best to restrain his laughter, lest he wind up on the receiving end of another hard slap. Nonetheless he was very amused, especially when he noticed the teacher's mixed reaction. On one hand, Ted had finally, after all those years, pronounced a word correctly. On the other hand, did it have to be *that* word?

Neither Ted nor my father would ever forget that special breakthrough, and they would laugh about it years later. On one such occasion, my dad visited Ted and found that he had a new dog. Ted explained how irked he was because his wife gave the dog a name he couldn't pronounce (yes, you can see where this is going). Ted, against his wife's wishes, went ahead and called the dog the only thing he could call it.

"Watch this," signed Ted, with a mischievous smile on his face. He took a deep breath.

"Fuck!"

Sure enough, the pooch came bouncing in, tail wagging affectionately. Never mind that the dog already knew how to respond to several commands *in sign language*. It was only one word, but it was Ted's biggest triumph from his school days.

Several years after all of these antics went on, PSD had a change of philosophy. Sometime in the early 1970's, they switched to the use of Total Communication in the classroom, using whichever communication method fit the needs of the students. Most teachers, in my opinion, appeared to use Sim-Com. This involved utilizing spoken words that were supported by their corresponding signs. It was not fluent ASL, but it was a step in the right direction. Students were getting a lot more information than they ever had (later, a teacher who had been at PSD during both the oral and the TC days would confide to me that the students indeed picked up educational content much faster when sign language was implemented).

Further down the road, PSD would eventually adopt a strong philosophy supporting the use of ASL in the classroom, and they would take many other steps to close the communication gap (such as implementing a successful Early Intervention program). At the point in time when I wanted to transfer, however, the gap was still very big. For even if PSD had improved its communication philosophy in school, there was nothing much it could do to improve things for the students at home and in the outside world, where they missed out on so much information. It was still a formidable game of catch-up.

Once my father was through explaining all of the previous dynamics involving the hardships of deaf education, he pointed out that I was lucky to get such a wonderful opportunity at GFS. I was lucky to have had enough residual hearing to establish a strong language base before I went deaf, and I was lucky to have supportive

Deaf parents after I did. I was lucky to have the cognitive skills to be able to survive at GFS. If he had been given such a choice, my father would have gone with GFS hands down (no pun intended). The education of deaf children still had a long way to go, he explained, so I might as well take advantage of my ability to succeed at GFS. If I had what it took to just barely make it, and it looked like I did, why not just hang in there? Maybe, someday, I would learn enough to help turn things around in the deaf world. For now, though, the deaf world would have to wait. I wasn't joining it just yet.

After the unsuccessful attempt at convincing my parents to let me transfer, I grudgingly returned to GFS. I cursed my luck. Why couldn't I have been prelingually deaf? Had I been born completely deaf, people would have left me alone. I wouldn't have been in this situation, trying to be the pseudo-hearing person I was. I didn't fit into the hearing world, and I wasn't allowed to be part of the Deaf world. I was too different.

And as my year in the eighth grade drew to a close, I had done it again: using mirrors, smokescreens and the deadly martial art of Bluff Yu, I gave the impression that I knew and understood most of what was going on around me. It was getting tiresome, however. I especially dreaded Wednesday assemblies, where I would sit there bored out of my mind while someone gave a speech, presentation or musical performance. Why didn't I just speak up and tell everyone that it was a waste of time for me? Of course, I never complained *(good boy, be hearing)*.

However, If my smile-when-everyone-smiles, laugh-when-everyone-laughs routine gave enough people the impression that I was hearing (or reasonably close enough), it didn't fool everyone. My teachers were no idiots, and they were observing me all along. They knew

I was getting by in my own way, but they also knew it wasn't going to last much longer. While the seventh and eighth grades consisted of mostly hands-on work and following textbook assignments, the ninth through twelfth grades were a whole new ballgame. In those upper grades, there would be an emphasis on classroom discussion. Instead of the teacher lecturing and leading us through textbook questions that were easier for me to follow, the whole class would be discussing topics in depth. We would all be learning from each other... except me.

The teachers, however, knew that I was really going to be in a fog if I had to follow an entire classroom discussion. They realized that if I were to remain at GFS, I would need some kind of extra support. Some consultation was done, and my mother gave me the news over the summer: I was going to get a sign-language interpreter. My reaction left no doubt about how I felt:

"Noooooooooooooooooooo!!!!"

I went into a big funk over this. It was bad enough that on many occasions, I had made a fool out of myself trying to act like I knew what was going on around me. I had become a world-champion nodder, saying yes to a lot of things people said in casual conversation. My personal rule was to always say "I don't know" to the teachers and "yeah" to the students when I couldn't understand anything. I thought I blended in better this way.

"Hey, whaddaya think about biology?"

(smiling) "Yeah!"

"Hey Mark, what time you got gym today?"

(smiling) "Yeah!"

"Hey Mark, wanna lick an ashtray?"

(smiling) "Yeah!"

Despite such incidents, I still believed that most of the time, I managed to blend in. With an interpreter, though, I was screwed. *Everyone* would see, every minute of every day, that I was deaf. There was no hiding from this fact, and I knew it. Everyone would be looking at me like I was the class freak. I was incredibly self-conscious about this and my self-esteem was at an all-time low.

Shortly before the end of my year in the eighth grade, it was also announced to me that I was being referred to a psychologist. My grade advisor had noted my behavior and obviously low self-esteem; he had seen enough to know that such a referral was necessary. Of course, I protested. My mother got the brunt of this. She had to put up with my ranting and raving:

"What am I, nuts? I'm not going to any psychologist. They're for people who are sick in the head. Booga booga booga... do I look sick to you? Oh, come on. They're just sending me there because I'm deaf. They think I'm deaf and dumb. I don't need any help..."

On and on I went, to no avail. My mother had to drag me there, but off to the psychologist I went.

My first session with the psychologist did not turn out to be the headshrinking, brainpicking session I feared it would be. As self-conscious as I was, I just couldn't stand the thought of being with a person whose sole purpose was to analyze me. My fear immediately turned into a sense of comfort and relief, though, when I found that my psychologist was a caring woman who signed. Seeing that she could sign fluently and understood deafness meant so much to me. I relaxed, and my initial streak of rebelliousness evaporated.

After some small talk and getting to know each other, I was asked to go through some psychological evaluation tests. I went through the usual battery of tests that measured my academic levels as well as my psychological wellbeing. At first I was apprehensive about this, but the psychologist made me feel better by explaining in detail why she had to run me through the whole thing. It meant a lot to me to be able to know exactly what was going on.

"You mean I have to do this to rule out the fact that I might be nuts?" I asked. She grinned, reassured me that I wasn't nuts, and we went on with the testing. As we went through it, I actually began to have fun. I knew I was doing well... I just enjoyed it as an opportunity to show off what I could do.

The following week, I beamed with pride as the psychologist told me that my test results were way above average. In fact, she added that she wasn't even sure I needed to see her much longer; she remarked that she could see how I had accomplished so much, against incredible odds, on my own. All I really needed, in her opinion, was a pat on the back. Then we moved on to talking about what was going on in school and with my family. I got a lot off my chest: the pressure of trying to be like a hearing person...the embarrassment when I couldn't... being made fun of... and wishing I could be with people like myself.

The psychologist acknowledged all of my concerns. For good measure, she told me that she would go over a few things with my family. She had observed that what my grandfather had told her about me was completely different from what she had seen with her own eyes. My grandfather had painted a bleak picture of how I was not good enough at several things, particularly speech. The psychologist informed me that my speech was far better than what she had expected, based on what my grandfather told her, but that was irrelevant. The important thing was that my grandparents needed to acknowledge that I was deaf, and that I was doing incredibly well considering the circumstances. My grades were better than a lot of hearing students, but to my grandfather it wasn't enough. During report card time, he would grill me on every teacher's written comments about how I needed to sit up closer, wear my hearing aid more, and be more involved in class discussion. Never mind how good my grades were. I needed to be more hearing.

By no means am I advocating a parenting philosophy of "oh, don't be so hard on him, he's deaf." Anything but. In situations where a teacher reported that I didn't give enough effort on a certain project, or failed to study enough for a final exam, the admonitions I got for it were appropriately called for. But there were some reprimands that I did not deserve, reprimands that were based on the comments such as the following examples (actual quotes from some of my report cards):

"I would have liked seeing Mark make greater contribution to class discussion."

"...he does not keep track of where we are in discussion."

"...I urge Mark to sit up front, focus his attention..."

Although there were many positive comments in my report cards where the teachers acknowledged I was overcoming a lot of adversity, my grandfather always gave me a hard time about my lack of involvement in class discussion. Sure, I'm grateful he pushed me hard academically, for it enabled me to set higher standards for myself; his only mistake was pushing for me to be more hearing. That would accomplish nothing, except for maybe turning me into a neurotic.

And then... shortly before the ninth grade began, I was at my grandparent's apartment when my grandfather called me into the den for yet another private conversation. We'd had countless meetings like this before, and I grew to detest them. But this time, it was different.

"Mark," he began. "This year is going to be a challenge for you. You've got a lot going on, but you've accomplished more than many people thought possible. I just wanted to say that you've proven yourself quite well. I'm not going to bother you anymore about GFS... you're on your own now."

I was completely surprised. It was a complete turnaround from what I would have expected from him. Although in general he was a fun guy to be with, as far as school was concerned he had always been dead serious. Perhaps he felt that I needed to be ten times better than everyone else in order to compensate for my deafness. Whatever it was, it was a big, unexpected surprise when he told me I was on my own. If I had any problems and needed advice, of course he would be there. If I ever turned in a lousy report card, then it would be up to my Deaf parents to say something (as it should be). Now my grandfather could go back to being just that: a grandfather. The same went for my grandmother, who had also shown a considerable amount of worry and concern over my academics. Our relationship greatly improved after this announcement, and I could go back to enjoying their company without rolling my eyes whenever a school-related issue came up.

When I rode back home with my mother that afternoon, she explained the reason behind what just happened. The psychologist had actually called my grandfather for a private discussion of their own. Basically, she told him to wake up and smell the roses. He was so worried about my deafness, that he had failed to see the big picture: overall, I was doing pretty well. With all that said and done, I felt vindicated.

"See? I *told* you I wasn't nuts."

Now that I could move on and face further academic challenges that awaited me at GFS, there was one more obstacle I needed to deal with myself. Despite reassurances from various adults, I still wasn't comfortable with the idea of having a sign language interpreter in class. I still felt very self-conscious about this, and wasn't ready for it yet. Luckily for me, I got a brief reprieve. Due to some red-tape snafu, an interpreter was not immediately available when the ninth grade began. It gave me time to assess the situation, the people around me, and how we would all respond to this person who would be following me around like a parole officer. It also gave me more time to struggle with my deafness alone.

And struggle with my deafness I did, in strange ways indeed. I immediately found out that the required ninth grade music class was not going to be the piece of cake I thought it would be. Previously, from third grade at Plymouth Meeting up to eighth grade at GFS, I could bluff my way through choir. I had enough residual hearing so that with a music sheet, I could learn the words to most songs. My nerve deafness was such that everyone's voice was garbled to me, but with the lyrics in my hand, I knew in advance what everyone would be saying. This enabled me to make the connection, and I could follow the music well enough to learn the words and lip-synch them as the class sang. I didn't mind doing this, really; sometimes, it was actually fun, especially at PMFS when we gave performances for parents and friends.

Ninth grade, though, was a different story. This was the big leagues. Instead of one class of fifteen kids singing together, the ninth grade choir was the entire class. All 104 of us. To make matters worse, the teachers split us up into different sections: tenor, bass, soprano, and terrified deaf kid. I was completely lost. There was no way I could keep up with all of this. After attending about three classes, I gave up. From there on, I cut weekly choir class, choosing instead to hide in some remote spot in the library. I would spend that time catching up on homework and hoping I wouldn't get in trouble for cutting choir. When the ninth grade gave a performance during an assembly, I sheepishly sat with the eighth graders, hoping no one would notice me.

Again, we have a similar issue reappearing here: why didn't I speak up? I could have, and should have, told them that it was crazy to put a deaf guy in a large choir class. Who would dispute that? What were they gonna do, put me up front and make me do a Pavarotti imitation? But no, I was convinced that because I was isolated in the hearing world, I had to play by the hearing rules. I never complained.

Finally, after a couple of months, I was informed that an interpreter would soon be assigned to me. This was it. All fingers would be pointed at me. *See that guy? He's deaf.* They were all going to make fun of me, I knew it. The weekend before I was scheduled to get my interpreter, I decided to pick up the school directory. I was going to sift through the names so that I could assess who would be most likely to ridicule me. This way, I would be prepared to deal with whatever embarrassment I knew was coming. I began to shuffle through the pages.

"Allen... nahhh. Brown... nahhh." A few minutes later it was "Zimmerman... nahhh." Suddenly, it dawned on me. Because of communication barriers, I wasn't really close to that many people, but no one out there was making my life miserable, either. They were pretty much leaving me alone. It was not they, the other students, but I myself who needed to come to terms with my deafness. I realized I was being too self-conscious. I decided I would give them a chance to see who I really was, and most importantly, I was going to give myself a chance.

The following Monday, I was in my usual fog in history class. A stimulating classroom discussion was underway, but I was relegated to biting my nails and drawing doodles in my notebook. To give the teacher a sense that I was hanging in there as best as I could, I would occasionally look at whoever was talking. It might have looked like I was following the conversation, but in reality I was in my own world. *Two outs, bases loaded... it's the bottom of the ninth, seventh game of the World Series... it doesn't get any better than this! Up to the plate steps Mark Drolsbaugh, the last hope for the Philadelphia Phillies... and here's the pitch...*

My daydream was suddenly interrupted by the class advisor, who walked into the room with another adult. He pointed towards me, and all of a sudden I had this woman pulling up a chair and sitting next to me. What the hell was this? She was right in my face, slowly enunciating with her lips every word of the classroom discussion. I was utterly confused. Where was the sign language? They hired some idiot who slowly repeated everything with exaggerated lip movements! And she did this while leaning so close to me that we looked like two lovesick teenagers sharing a sundae in some '50's malt shop. My face reddened with embarrassment as I put up with this cheap imitation of an interpreter for another half-hour. I could feel the rest of the class sneaking glances at us and wondering, *what the hell is that?*

Mercifully, the class came to an end and my interpreter was formally able to introduce herself.

"Hi, my name is Emily... sorry I was late, but I spoke with your advisor for a while and will be working with you from now on." She was really nice, but...

"Hi," I said, somewhat hesitantly. Then I began to sign slowly, "nice to meet you."

Emily's eyes widened in astonishment. Signing fluently, she said, "*You sign?* Oh my god! No one told me! This is unbelievable!" She dropped her head on the desk and began laughing. Looking up, she explained that she had been given the impression that I was a total oralist who did not know any sign language whatsoever. I explained to her that I was never encouraged to sign, but was able to gradually pick up ASL from my parents and my friends at PSD. Emily shook her head, smiling, and we laughed at the whole thing. We continued signing to each other and I realized that for the first time in my career at GFS, I was having a lengthy, meaningful conversation with someone.

At the next class, Emily was signing full speed ahead, and the entire class was mesmerized. The beauty of ASL was there for all to see... graceful, flowing hands relaying tons of information to me. There was certainly nothing to be embarrassed about as far as I was concerned. In fact, I was too much in awe of all the information that was coming in. Wonder of wonders, I found that my classmates were pretty cool people, after all! I suddenly had access to their classroom discussion as well as their casual conversation and jokes. For the first time, I could understand everything that was going on around me and could appreciate everyone's input. You know how they say two minds are better than one? Well, I suddenly had access to 104 minds, and it was a veritable orgy of information. How could I have gone for so long while missing out on so much?

My life had changed incredibly for the better after I got the interpreter. The same went for my teachers, who knew they could now treat me as an equal; the old "duhhh, I didn't know there was a homework assignment" excuse didn't work anymore. I was in on everything, and benefited from it immensely. Not only was I expected to improve my work (I did), but I was also expected to be involved in classroom discussion (I was). Other students developed a better understanding of what I was like, and they realized why I had appeared so lost (not to mention weird) in earlier times. Some of them were so impressed with sign language that they took it upon themselves to try learning some. A number of those students learned enough so that they could hold a very basic conversation in ASL, although most just learned how to fingerspell the alphabet. Whether it was signing words or fingerspelling them, it meant a lot to me. It was great to see how a number of students were eager to understand my world.

One such student, Erik, helped other students become more sensitive to my needs. One day I was sitting with a small group of classmates in the cafeteria, and I was completely out of it. There was just no way I could keep up with the conversation. Erik eventually joined us at our table and he noticed right away that I was not involved in the conversation. First he briefly took on the role of interpreter, as he summarized the content of the discussion which was taking place. It didn't appeal to either of us, so we started having our own conversation in ASL while the others continued speaking. Suddenly, one of the students sitting next to Erik began to protest.

"Hey," he began. "It's not fair when you two sign like that... I can't understand what you're saying."

Erik couldn't believe this. He shot back with an incredulous look.

"How do you think *Mark* feels, twenty-four hours a day, when he can't understand anything you and everyone else are saying?"

The object of Erik's wrath suddenly had a blank look on his face. It hit him... boom, massive insight in progress.

"Oh, man..."

Soon afterwards, this student learned sign language himself, as did a number of others at the table that day who caught wind of this sobering realization. When my interpreter heard about what happened, she broke into a big grin. She knew we were all learning something new. In a while, a number of students would be asking her for feedback on their signing skills. This whole thing was a blessing for me, indeed.

Obviously, I could breathe easier once I had the services of an interpreter. Unfortunately, Emily had to move out of town, but another interpreter, Deborah, was hired in her place. Not only was Deb as fluent in ASL, but she was well versed in anything related to the deaf community as well. It was strange, but here was this hearing person teaching me, a deaf guy, everything I ever wanted to know about ASL and Deaf culture. We would talk about it, and she would point out things about deafness which I never had the time or maturity to realize myself. In addition, I noticed that having an interpreter around actually improved my own sign language skills, as I was being exposed to ASL on a daily basis. I was learning more about myself and enjoying my education as well.

I was, for a change, experiencing the joys of going to school, and I have many good memories of my junior and senior years. Perhaps one of the funniest stories was the time Mr. Gratwick, my eleventh grade history teacher, held me after class. History was always my worst subject, and it was kind of awkward for me because Mr. Gratwick was also the varsity baseball coach. It was a schizophrenic relationship that year; I dreaded him during the morning, loved him in the afternoon. One day, history class had just ended and I began to grab my books and leave. Mr. Gratwick then approached me and asked if I could stay for a few minutes. I groaned, knowing how I had bombed on a recent assignment. Instead, to my surprise, this after-class meeting was about baseball.

"Mark," Mr. Gratwick began, "I need to go over something which happened in yesterday's game." My eyes lit up... for baseball, I had all the time in the world.

"When you were at bat with Tommy on third, I gave you the signal for a safety squeeze bunt. You missed it, and Tommy nearly got picked off. You sure you know what the bunt sign is?" I acknowledged that I did, but in that specific situation I must have been distracted or something. I just missed it. Mr. Gratwick said it was no problem, I just had to make sure to be alert for any signals he might give while I was at bat. Then he broke into a big grin.

"You, of all people, missing a sign..."

Now that I was all settled down at GFS, enjoying school for a change, it was time to move on to other things in life. Namely, growing up. Meeting girls. Getting a life. Thanks to my interpreter at school and baseball at home, getting a life was the easy part. I had a number of new friends at school who accepted me for who I was, and at home I grew closer to friends whom I spent entire summers playing baseball with.

Meeting girls, however, was a total bust for me. Yes, there were a number of girls who would say hi to me or even be platonic friends with me, but none of them wanted anything beyond that. I was the nice deaf guy; fun to talk to, nice to get to know a bit better, but not the kind of guy you would want to bring home with you. I'm not sure what it was. Maybe no one wanted to date a deaf guy, because all the girls were supposed to go out with popular jocks. Maybe some girls were actually interested, but afraid to get close to someone who was so different. Maybe it was my weird sense of humor. I'll never know.

Whatever it was, it got frustrating at times... I would see lots of guys getting all the girls they wanted, dating one after the other. Not me. In some ways, this was a blessing; someday, when pigs flew and hell froze over, I would have a girlfriend... and when I did, I would be ten times nicer than most guys. I would appreciate it more, instead of taking women for granted like many guys did.

Finally, one day a pig flew by my window and a girl named Karen asked me if I would accompany her to her junior prom. It caught me totally off guard; she was not from GFS, I didn't really know her, and she asked me out of the blue. She was the friend of the girlfriend of a good friend of mine, and she heard I was available. She must have figured I was worth a shot. Further throwing me for a loop was the fact that prior to asking me to do this, she had practiced repeatedly until she could ask in sign language. Who was this girl? Why me, why now? Why not? I said yes. It had been too long since I had an opportunity like this.

It was definitely worth the wait, as we had a great time at the prom and kept seeing each other for a long time afterwards. It turned out to be another lesson in life for me, one that I initially could not understand. Of course, my parents were elated that I finally had a girlfriend; my dad was glad to know that I wasn't the eunuch he thought I was, and my mom was absolutely thrilled that there was someone for me who knew sign language. As long as Karen could sign, that was all that mattered. Unfortunately, the rest of my family was not as receptive. Karen was a fluent signer, yes, but she was also Catholic. Needless to say, they were not too thrilled about this and they let me know it.

All of this had me terribly confused. After years of being dateless, I finally found someone who not only wanted to know me on an intimate level, but also knew sign language to boot. Was I supposed to throw it all away just because she was Catholic? I didn't understand the big deal. This was going to be a lesson for me similar to the one I learned while growing up with Sekou; why should anyone's religion or race make a difference in how we get along? Neither religion nor race mattered to me; communication did. If you were willing to be my friend and accept my deafness, I didn't care if you were white, black, Catholic, Jewish, Swahili or whatever. I didn't care if you worked as a CEO or passed your time handing out flowers at the airport. If you can *communicate*, you're my friend. This is one incidence in where I feel my deafness has helped me grow spiritually... I could appreciate my interaction with anyone and just be happy we could get along, rather than being hung up on what groups or religion they belonged to. Really, human interaction is a blessing; it's such a waste to discriminate.

While I was coming to terms with my hearing family's initial reaction to Karen's background (they eventually warmed up to her), I took advantage of the opportunity to find out just what the big deal was supposed to be. Out of curiosity, I began attending church with Karen. It was a brand new experience, and it was beautiful. My parents didn't really object, but they were concerned that it would greatly upset my mother's family. I agreed with them on that, so I never mentioned it to anyone other than my parents. It was my business. If Karen could jump so deeply into my world of sign language, I could likewise jump into her world of Catholicism. Why not? We should all learn from one another. I believe I had a really good thing going. Both Judaism and Catholicism are beautiful religions, and I could experience both. Hanukkah, Christmas, the whole shebang. Besides, I had already celebrated Christmas on many occasions with my father's family. How could it hurt if I was involved with one more? I had the best of both worlds.

As it turned out, I enjoyed going to church, and I learned a lot from it. What really helped was the fact that Karen would discreetly interpret everything into sign language for me. I had access, and I was fascinated. Not only was I struck by the differences between Catholicism and Judaism, but even more so by their similarities. There were common threads everywhere, and I was picking them up every week. It reinforced a sense that somehow, we're all in this together.

My only problem with religion, then, was the confusion I felt after seeing so many people making a fuss over religious differences. I never mentioned my church experiences to my Jewish family, for I had seen their reservations about my dating a Catholic girl. Likewise, I rarely talked about Jewish culture in the presence of Catholics, for I had noticed a sense of anti-Semitism in certain individuals. Maybe it was just me, but I had felt a distinctive sense of us vs. them. Although most of the people and most of the experiences were overwhelmingly positive, there were always people on each side making derogatory comments about other faiths. Whenever this happened, I instinctively knew it was wrong. Both religions, in my opinion, were beautiful in their own right. I guess we all have an individual responsibility to learn tolerance and respect for each other. Until that happens, we all have a long way to go.

In a strange way, I'm actually glad I'm deaf. Perhaps if I weren't deaf, I might have developed a true bias favoring the first religion I was exposed to. Perhaps if I were hearing, the first morsel of religious dogma thrown my way might have been unconditionally accepted as Absolute Truth. But no, I was deaf... and I grew up with a blank slate that enabled me to look at things from a more neutral perspective. In other words, deafness emptied my cup. It has allowed me to see different religions simply as they are, without any bias. It has helped me learn, and I literally thank God for deafness.

Karen and I had a long relationship, dating each other exclusively for about three years. Three years! Normally three years is not much, but when those years are ages sixteen, seventeen and eighteen, it's an eternity. In all honesty, our relationship stretched out for far too long. One year, maximum, probably would have been more ideal. The years sixteen, seventeen and eighteen are best suited for dating lots of people, socializing, and learning the responsibilities which come with approaching adulthood.

For Karen and myself, it was a different story. Whereas other teenage couples routinely broke up and found new dates to go out with, I held on to Karen with a vise grip. After all, she was the only girl in the whole neighborhood who signed. If we broke up, I knew it would take me years to find another language-accessible girlfriend. So I held on to her, through good times and bad. Sometimes, near the end of our relationship, we could hardly tolerate each other, but I just couldn't let go. Karen, in turn, had to put up with my periodic, insecure bouts of jealousy. I always felt that hearing guys had more to offer her than I did, and I didn't want her to realize it. As it turned out, Karen was ready to break free, but she also felt bad for me. I could understand her mixed emotions.

The end came after Karen enrolled in a local college. After years of being in an all-girls' high school, she was surrounded by other men for the first time in her life. They were hearing, like her, and shared similar interests in music and entertainment that I could not. In fact, Karen remarked frequently that she felt guilty whenever we went to the movies, because she knew she could never fully interpret the mood and context that was taking place on the screen. Likewise, I would spend hours in movie theaters pretending I was enjoying every moment, because I wanted her to be happy. It was not fair to either of us. We knew it had to end, and we appropriately broke up. For Karen, it meant she was free at last. For me, it meant the same thing, although I didn't know it yet.

Breaking up with Karen was nothing compared to a lot of other things that were going on. The mid-eighties were quite a period transition for me. In the spring of 1984, I was a senior at GFS and on track to graduate. The first deaf student ever to graduate from GFS! Sadly, though, Grandpop was losing a battle against cancer. He was hospitalized in such bad shape that we weren't sure he would last long enough to see me graduate... it was his big dream for me that I would make it at GFS. It was something he bragged about to everyone: a well-to-do surgeon told him I'd never make it at GFS, and here I was completing my senior year.

By late April, we knew for sure that he wasn't going to around much longer. More than anything, I wanted him to know that a GFS diploma was in the bag and that I did it for him. Approaching him in his hospital room, I informed him that not only was I going to graduate in June, but had also been accepted into Temple University. I also told him I was going to be an accountant. I have no idea why I said that. I guess it seemed the thing to do. Everyone else in my hearing family was a successful doctor, lawyer, accountant or teacher; I didn't want to give him the impression that I had no idea what I wanted to do. I thought it would be best to let him die happy knowing that I not only graduated GFS, but had a prospective career in business awaiting.

Finally, on May fourth 1984, my dad woke me up at six a.m. with the devastating news: Grandpop had passed on. The most spiritual person I had ever known was gone. After a brief trip to the hospital with the family, I returned to GFS around noon, totally numb from the immeasurable loss. It was just too surreal... I couldn't believe Grandpop had died. As shell-shocked as I was, there was still a baseball game to be played later on that day against powerful Archbishop Ryan. I wasn't sure if I should play or not, but then I recalled how Grandpop had always been a familiar face at many of my games. He was my biggest fan, always cheering me on. So that was settled... I was going to play this one hard for him.

When the game rolled around, Archbishop Ryan jumped to a big lead in the first two innings. They were up 5-0 when Mr. Gratwick decided to pull our starting pitcher and put me on the mound. This was clearly the strongest team we had to play all year and we were outmatched that day. Nonetheless, I pitched five innings, getting seven strikeouts while giving up only two earned runs. While I may have had better statistics in other games, I would say this was the best I had ever pitched in my life, considering the circumstances and the talent level of the other team. We lost, but we improved mightily and won the Friends' League Championship a few weeks later with a 19-4 record. And shortly afterward, I had a diploma in my hand. This one's for you, Grandpop.

Of course, I would miss Grandpop terribly. I had lost my greatest role model of all time, one of very few people I could really look up to. Granted, there was much he did not understand about deafness, but he made up for it in so many other ways.

I considered myself blessed to have had such a wonderful grandfather, and in contemplating that, I realized that there was much I had taken for granted. Naturally, there were many things I wished I could have done all over again, things that I would have either appreciated more or done better. With that in mind, I decided I would make the most of the time I had left with my surviving grandparents.

Considering that my dad's mother, Nana, had moved from Scranton to an apartment in nearby Hatboro (with her second husband Mike Novak), I took advantage of the opportunity to visit often. Most of the time, I would accompany my parents to visit Nana and Mike, often during alternate weekends and during holidays such as Christmas and Easter. After Grandpop died, however, I got into the habit of driving over myself just to say hello and shoot the breeze.

I might have been a young adolescent barely old enough to have a driver's license, but I still noticed that there were certain differences in family dynamics that stood out when I interacted with my Deaf grandparents. For instance, I was incredibly relaxed with them. It was just kicking back, no pressure. No struggling to read lips. No need to act like a hearing person. There were no reminders that I needed to speak more clearly or wear a hearing aid. With Nana and Mike, this was not necessary. They were Deaf themselves... they *understood*.

If I told them about a time I completely screwed up in class, they would acknowledge that it must have been hard for me (hearing relatives usually told me it was my responsibility to sit up front). If it was something amusing, such as the time I said "I don't know" to the substitute teacher who asked what my name was, Nana and Mike laughed along with me. I appreciated this because although there are many situations where there's nothing more we can do but laugh at ourselves, deafness was no laughing matter for my hearing family. Worrying about me to a fault, they would react with grave concern and repeatedly point out that I needed to make certain adjustments to survive in the hearing world.

To Nana and Mike, however, deafness was something we were, not something that needed to be fixed. Consequently, I never felt like I needed to win their approval. Nana and Mike didn't care if I wore a hearing aid; they didn't care if I could speak clearly or not. They didn't worry incessantly about things that were out of our control. There was no you should know this, you should do that. Whoever I was at that particular moment in time was just fine with them. The important thing was that I was doing okay in whatever way I could.

Another benefit of having Deaf family was that with them, there was no "Dinner Table Syndrome" where the deaf person sits completely lost amongst the hearing family members having a table conversation. So it was not uncommon for my parents and I to stay for a duration which would have been unbearable with hearing people. Time flew, because everyone was involved fully in whatever was going on.

One evening in 1985, I had just paid a visit to my Deaf grandparents and had enjoyed a lengthy stay. Around ten p.m. I figured it was time to call it a night, so I said goodbye and headed out to the parking lot. As I pulled out of my parking space, I looked up towards the apartment building. I could see Nana standing by the window of the eighth floor lobby, waving goodbye. I waved back, and as I left the lot, I found myself overcome with emotion. For whatever reason, I was all choked up, tears streaming down my face.

Call it uncanny, call me weird, but something unusual happened that night. I really believe that somehow, Nana and I both knew that it was the last time things would be the way they were. I couldn't understand for the life of me why I started sniffling when she waved goodbye. But somehow, deep down, I knew. And I believe that somehow, Nana knew it too. She had never walked to the lobby and waved from that window before. A sense of imminent change overwhelmed me.

The following day, I had my answer. The phone rang, and it was a relative calling to inform us that Nana had suffered a serious stroke. She would never be the same again. Visiting her in the hospital, my family and I discovered that she was unable to walk, unable to use her right hand, had lost her ability to read, and was confusing various family member's names with each other. She referred to my dad as "Robert,"and Uncle Bob as "Charlie." She was in for a long period of rehabilitation.

As often as I could, I visited Nana in the hospital. Perhaps I felt guilty because when my grandfather was terminally ill, I was not always there for him. It was impossible for me to be involved as much as I would have liked. I recall one time, when Grandpop was close to death, an uncle urged me,

"Go ahead, speak to Grandpop. Go ahead, say something." Feeling pressured, awkward and uncomfortable, I leaned over to his bed. He was obviously in bad shape and would not be around much longer.

"So," I began. "How ya doing?" Grandpop, too weak to talk, rolled his eyes as if to say "well, duhhhh." I actually smiled, because knowing him, what he meant to say was "oh come on, I taught you to be wiser than this. Say what comes from your heart, not what others want you to."

Now that it was Nana who was sick, I was saying the things that came from my heart. Perhaps I was more mature this time around, or perhaps I was more comfortable around Deaf relatives. We openly shared stories with Nana, and we discussed her progress with the doctors. With Grandpop, I was often in the dark as far as what the doctors and relatives were saying. Sometimes I felt like a burden, for it was hard enough for the hearing family to deal with Grandpop's illness without having to slowly repeat all the grim news to me. With Nana, however, most of us were Deaf so we all shared the medical prognosis together on the same wavelength. We had the whole story, which was that she had quite an uphill battle to fight.

Slowly, Nana began to make enough progress so that she could be discharged from the hospital. However, before returning home, she would have to spend some time in a rehabilitation center, which turned out to be Hopkins House in Jenkintown. It was a fine facility, and Nana did indeed make some progress. She slowly regained her ability to walk, although she would still need to spend much time in a wheelchair. Everything else, however, was coming along slowly. Her right hand was still curled up, unable to function properly. She complained that she could no longer read books or follow the captions on TV. Interestingly, her signing skills remained intact, although she was limited to signing with one hand (a report in *Time* magazine several years later would confirm that sign language stimulates different areas of the brain than the ones activated by spoken and written language).

Shortly after returning home, Nana had yet another setback. She collapsed from a second stroke, and Mike was barely able to assist her in time to save her life. After another hospital stay, it was determined that Nana would need to live in a place where she would have round-the-clock medical supervision. Grudgingly, she and Mike accepted the family's strong recommendation that they move to the Nevil Home, a nursing home for the deaf in Media, Pennsylvania.

Of course, no couple likes to leave the freedom of their own place to live in... a home. A retirement community. Nana might have lost some function, but her wit was intact:

"Put me out to pasture, eh? Why not take me behind the barn and shoot me?"

Soon, however, Nana and Mike were settled down... and having a great time. There were nightly events such as movies, games, and occasional trips such as an excursion to Atlantic City. The other residents were Deaf, and the staff signed, so Nana and Mike were actually socializing a whole lot more than they ever did at their old apartment complex. Nana had somewhat regained that spark she was missing... she began to hurl friendly insults at Mike, even throwing the Kleenex box at him whenever he dozed off in front of the TV. When she started making fun of other people and cracking one-liners, a la the Sophia character on *The Golden Girls*, that's when I knew she was on her way back. She would jokingly complain that Mike had a roving eye for the other ladies, that he was trying to turn the place into a swingers club. Mike would play along mischievously, making catcalls whenever a female resident walked by their room. It became one big party, getting to the point where our family would smuggle in beer and whiskey for Mike. It wasn't permitted, but so what. If these were the twilight years, why shouldn't they enjoy every minute of it?

Although Nana would never be the same as she was before the strokes, I could tell that she was making much progress at the Nevil Home. I couldn't help but take note of it... at the Hopkins House, she was surrounded by the most professional, competent staff of physical therapists you could ever ask for, yet her heart wasn't really in it. She made enough progress to go home, but just barely. At the Nevil Home, Nana was enjoying life again, socializing with her Deaf peers, and her spirits rose remarkably high enough that she was able to bounce back considerably from her stroke. I really believe that having Deaf friends, family and staff around gave Nana the emotional boost that enabled her to regain much of what she had lost.

After settling down at the Nevil Home, it wasn't long before she was once again able to read and do her favorite crossword puzzles. She still had to spend much time in a wheelchair, and she also continued to struggle with her short-term memory, but she had nonetheless come a long way. The bottom line was that she once again was enjoying a quality of life she hadn't experienced since her days as the cook at a local Deaf club.

If you stop to think about it, you'll notice a parallel here: often, people have argued that deaf children so rightly deserve a quality of life which is available only through permitting them to interact with their deaf peers. In this case, with Nana and Mike, I had discovered that it was a universal truth that applied to all ages (ironically, I had yet to realize that this truth applied to me as well). The Nevil home had allowed them to find that missing spark, a spark that gave them strength to recover physically, emotionally and spiritually.

Nana and Mike would spend the next seven years in the Nevil Home, where the family would get together to celebrate Christmas and other joyous occasions on a regular basis. When they both eventually passed away (within months of each other, Nana in the fall of 1991 and Mike in the spring of 1992), we had accumulated many wonderful memories. Interestingly, when they passed away, I did not grieve as hard as I did when Grandpop died in 1984. Maybe it was because Grandpop had such a powerful influence on me that it was like losing a part of myself. Maybe it was because Nana and Mike had often frankly discussed with the family how they were ready to die... it gave us all an opportunity to make the most of the final years and to have closure. Nana and Mike gave us all plenty of time to say what needed to be said and do what needed to be done. It was like a peaceful send-off to the next world for them. So perhaps we were more prepared to deal with their departure. Either way, I do miss them very much and consider myself blessed to have had such wonderful grandparents on both sides of the family.

Chapter 6

Despite graduating from what was one of the best schools in Philadelphia, somewhere down the line I forgot to pat myself on the back. My self-esteem, somehow, was pretty low. I had graduated from a school where many graduates went on to success in Ivy League colleges, but I didn't dare dream of such lofty ideals. Rather than Doogie Howser, M.D., I was going to be Bud Bundy or Bart Simpson. For as much as I knew I had survived one of the toughest academic environments in town, I hadn't seen any other deaf role models around.

Apparently, being the first deaf guy to graduate from GFS had positive and negative implications. On one hand, I had accomplished what was thought to be impossible, and that certainly was commendable. On the other hand, I had just blazed a path never before traveled... and I had no one to follow. Where did I go from there? I had no idea. My hearing classmates may have gone on to medical school or various prestigious positions in science, business and entertainment, but they were hearing. What was a deaf guy to do?

In a way, I was the victim of a self-imposed glass ceiling. I surmised that my hearing classmates were of course going to be successful, because they were hearing. They had the leadership qualities, I didn't. I may have improved after getting an interpreter, but I was still a few steps behind; being a leader was out of the question. If there were situations where a good idea was needed, someone else already came up with the solution by the time the problem was effectively communicated to me through the interpreter. Lots of times I would raise my hand two or three seconds after everyone else due to this small delay, and curse under my breath as some other student gave an opinion which was exactly what I had planned to bring up. I was close, but I was never equal.

Not being equal to anyone gave me an excuse to sell myself short, and I did. Breaking up with Karen further reinforced my belief that a deaf guy just didn't have much of a fair shot at succeeding in a hearing world. Although we managed to remain friends, it was painful at first to see all of the success Karen had meeting other men. She was having the time of her life dating hearing guys who had much more to offer her than I ever could, and I was back to striking out with the ladies. I was going nowhere fast. I had no dreams or aspirations. If I landed any job at all, be it flipping burgers at McDonalds or washing windshields with a squeegee at street intersections, it would be *not bad for a deaf guy.*

Eventually, I got a part-time job as a supermarket clerk. It was okay, nothing fancy. To me, it was the end of the road. Since this job was *not bad for a deaf guy*, I had made it my career goal. Maybe someday I would manage the general merchandise department... even if that never happened, I was still doing pretty good, because this was *not bad for a deaf guy.*

Needless to say, this was probably the low point of my life. Grandpop was gone, my love life had evaporated, and I was in a rut stocking the same shelves every day at work. There had to be more to life than this. Something was missing, and I grew tired of feeling like there was a big void in my life. If I had any guts, I would have uprooted and started all over someplace else. In fact, I mentioned this to some hearing friends of mine at a party somewhere around this time. I told them that I'd heard of this place called NTID (National Technical Institute for the Deaf) in Rochester, and I was thinking of going there. Perhaps it was time for me to move on and get to be with people like myself for a change. But it never happened. Not only were my friends able to talk me out of it, I don't think I was ready for such a move yet anyway. I was in a rut, but it was a *comfortable* rut in the hometown I had lived in all my life.

One of my friends told me that I didn't need to look elsewhere for happiness, I simply needed to look inwards and find more confidence. I needed to be more assertive, needed to believe in myself. Only then would things get better for me. He had a point there; I needed an attitude overhaul. After some soul-searching, I found an intriguing answer: the martial arts. This was not entirely new to me; I had taken Shotokan a few years back, and it left an indelible impression. I remembered how I always looked forward to class, and realized that the martial arts had this knack for filling a gap in my life. It was time to start up again. After checking out some of the schools in my neighborhood, I decided to enroll at a Tae Kwon Do school in nearby Willow Grove. Not surprisingly, it turned out to be a valuable experience.

First and foremost, Tae Kwon Do (as well as any other martial art) is physically relaxing and cathartic. If you have any pent-up stress or frustration, this is a great outlet. Not only do you release negative tension, but you also pick up positive vibes from your teachers and students when you work out in harmony. You also develop an ability to focus and stay tuned to the present moment, which is the key to inner peace. It does wonders for your state of mind. The difference in the way I carried myself around was noticeable. In fact, the two times I had to take an extended leave of absence from Tae Kwon Do (once for a hernia operation and again after a freak surfing accident), my boss at work observed a big difference in my usually calm demeanor. My tolerance level in difficult situations had waned somewhat compared to when I regularly participated in Tae Kwon Do.

On a different level, Tae Kwon Do improved my self-esteem. When I started training, I noticed that the advanced students looked awesome as they executed difficult techniques with smooth precision. I couldn't believe that someday, I too would be performing the same complex routines. Sure enough, as time went by, I improved, and I realized I could routinely accomplish what I once thought was impossible. It taught me to never say never.

If at this point it appears I'm getting too big for my britches regarding martial arts skills, hang on a second. That, too, is naturally taken care of by the rigors of training. When I was a green belt (about intermediate level), I began to think that I was the second coming of Bruce Lee. This is understandable because it is at this stage when beginners tend to become adept at all of the basic techniques. Instead of awkward, off-balance kicks, I began to deliver powerful blows with speed and accuracy. *Whoooooomp!* I could literally feel the energy surging within me. Damn, I was good. Or so I thought.

A while later, when I was a red belt (advanced level), I was warming up one day when I noticed one of the green belts going through his repertoire of kicks and punches.

"Hmmm," I thought. "He's pretty good, but he's got a long way to go."

All of a sudden, at that moment, it hit me. I realized that statement not only applied to the green belt, but to me as well. As a green belt I thought I knew everything, but as a red belt I knew in retrospect that I was wrong. Not only that, I realized that at the present moment, even as a red belt I still knew nothing compared to what was ahead. And of course, as a black belt, I would likewise know nothing compared to the path beyond. It was a humbling insight, one I am grateful for.

Once you get such insights from your training, it adds a spiritual dimension to your life. You begin to question the meaning of some things, and realize that you have a power deep inside you that you were never aware of before. I think we all have this power, and it lies dormant within us. We all have more ability and wisdom than we give ourselves credit for. Once I realized this, I became an Eastern Philosophy enthusiast, reading everything I could get my hands on about Zen Buddhism, Taoism, and various readings related to spirituality. I became a strong believer in the inner voice.

Ironically, during my school years, I had been cultivating an awareness of my inner voice all along. From third grade at PMFS through my senior year at GFS (both of which were Friends Schools of the Quaker background and philosophy), I had been a participant in weekly meeting for worship. This involved the whole school getting together in a meetinghouse, and sitting still doing nothing. It was a form of meditation that I would get into even more as a martial artist. The whole idea beyond this meeting for worship was that we all have "the light" within us. If, at any time someone had a brilliant inspiration, it was believed to come from God. If such an inspiration arose, one was encouraged to stand up and break the silence by sharing the inspiration with others.

After all of my experiences in Judaism and Catholicism, I realized that I blended in best with Quakerism. After all, there were no hard-set rules, no "you should do this, you should know that." Instead, we were encouraged to trust ourselves and the voice within. There is a little bit of God in each of us, and I still believe that to this day. I might be biased in this opinion, for an obvious reason. In Judaism and Catholicism, I was never an equal. In the meditative silence of Quakerism, we were all the same. No spiritual rank and order, no straining to understand what was going on. It was just sitting together in Oneness.

Obviously, my martial arts background further reinforced my Quaker experience. I also realized that in the past, I had already utilized my inner voice, when it warned me against the perils of discrimination. Somehow I knew it was wrong when my friend Sekou was treated unfairly because he was black, and I knew it was wrong when I heard anti-Semitic or anti-Catholic remarks about anyone. I vowed from there on that I would always trust my inner voice. It has never let me down.

Coming back to Earth and getting back to Tae Kwon Do, I eventually earned a black belt in the fall of 1990. At the time, it was my most memorable achievement to date. It was one of few things I had done entirely on my own. Just about everything else I had accomplished, someone else was pushing me along. Tae Kwon Do was a path I chose to pursue alone, by my own volition. There were times I would come home, exhausted, with an assortment of strains and sprains. Occasionally, family members would take note, shake their heads, and wonder out loud why I was putting myself through all of this. But the martial arts had succeeded in teaching me a valuable lesson; I learned that when we bear down and put our minds to it, we can accomplish anything.

What with all of the previous musings about religion and the martial arts, one might assume that it added a significant degree of wisdom and maturity to my life. Uh, yeah, maybe... but don't forget, I was still in my early twenties. I was still a fish out of water, a deaf person trying to blend in with hearing people. So of course I would continue making more mistakes and questionable decisions, especially during the first few years as a college student.

Both my academic and social lives during the college years had a certain schizophrenic quality to them. At Temple University, I was on academic probation one semester, and pulled in a 3.34 GPA the next. I was an accounting major one year, a psych major the next. Social life at the university was practically nil. There were too many faces, all of them hearing. My best friends were my interpreters, Alyx and Mike. Without them, I would have flunked out due to academic incompetence or total boredom, whichever came first.

At home, I hung out mostly the same group of friends I played baseball with. However, we were no longer the cute little ballplayers who won Little League, Pony League and Summer Rec League championships. These kids had grown up to become wild college students.

Hanging out with my buddies was always fun, especially before we turned twenty-one. Old enough to hang out but too young to hit the bars, we usually had to resort to sports for a good time. We would play baseball, basketball, touch football, and street hockey. When we were done with baseball, we joined organized softball leagues. We were forever young, at least until we hit twenty-one.

Once we were old enough to go to the clubs, something changed in the social dynamics. Previously, I could easily tolerate not always knowing what was being said whenever we were playing sports. I was having too much fun shooting baskets or hitting home runs to worry about missing some conversational tidbits. But it was a completely different story when we started hitting the bars. Rather than passing a ball around, my friends were just standing there, beer in hand, hoping to meet some nice women. I still had a lot of fun hanging out with them, but it was harder to interact. I could talk to anyone one-on-one, but once a group thing was going, I was lost. It would be fun one moment, excruciatingly boring the next.

To get through the boring interludes, I would order more drinks. If I was hopelessly out of a conversation, off to the bar I went. While everyone was talking, I was drinking. After seven or so beers, I would have a good buzz going, and would suddenly become the life of the party. Whether it was giving someone a wedgie, telling X-rated jokes or doing the old "pull my finger" routine, I had become an alcohol-driven animal.

During the summer months, it would get especially crazy. I would be swimming in beer. Every year, we would rent a summer house at the Jersey Shore, and the antics would begin. Initially we rented at Wildwood, but eventually toned down somewhat (for us) and got a place at more laid-back Long Beach Island. Hanging out with everyone at the beach was much more enjoyable than going to the bars with them in the city; I knew everyone well, we had fun on the beach, and we partied hard together in our beach house. Of course, I was always lost in group conversations, but nonetheless managed to find a way to have fun. Perhaps the best thing about it was that despite the occasional frustrations, I could still laugh at myself. Sometimes it was all I could do. One such incident that comes to mind occurred on the boardwalk in Wildwood:

On one hot sunny afternoon, I decided to go for a walk alone. It was a beautiful day, and I loved "hitting the boards" where all the stores and arcades were. I took off by myself, leaving behind a number of friends who had yet to wake up and recover from the partying they did the night before. Ah, what a beautiful day it was... strolling by myself, the sun shining brightly, glittery stores on my left and the waves of the ocean gently rolling on my right. Lots of beautiful women, too. In fact, they were looking at me. I nonchalantly strutted by, reveling in all of the attention. Obviously, they must have been admiring my muscular body (okay, so I had to suck in my gut a little bit, but so what). I grinned at the ladies, and the fact that their eyes were following me further inflated my adolescent, hormone-ravaged ego. Remember that scene in *Saturday Night Fever* where John Travolta strutted down the street to thumping disco music? Replace the leisure suit with Bermuda shorts and real groovy sunglasses, and that was me.

Soon, however, I got the feeling that something was not quite right. Another group of women began staring at me as I walked by, but I noticed it wasn't the kind of admiring glance my ego had deluded me into perceiving the first time around. Not only that, I immediately spotted a group of *guys* who were really giving me the eye.

"Waitaminute, something's wrong here," I thought. Instinctively, I turned around. Ohhhh, man. There was a tram car right on my heels, loaded with about fifty passengers. Not only was the driver beeping his horn and yelling at me to get out of the way, but I also learned that there was a loud, pre-recorded "watch the tram car, please" message blaring repeatedly over the speakers. My face turned bright red, and I felt like shrinking to the size of an ant and crawling under the boardwalk.

Aw, heck, what could I do? When I got back to the house, I told the guys what happened, and we all had a good laugh over it. For the rest of the summer, they would exaggeratingly tackle me or push me out of the way whenever a tram car was remotely in the vicinity. Sometimes, you just gotta laugh. Laugh and the world laughs with you, they say. Sure, sometimes they're laughing *at* you, but you've just gotta smile and move on.

In between partying it up at the beach and my academic endeavors at Temple, I managed to continue my successful career as a supermarket clerk. My salary had steadily risen over the four years I worked there (1984-1988), and I was given more responsibility. *Not bad for a deaf guy.* When I finished college, I could go full-time and get a life. Why not? I enjoyed the environment I was in, and most of the customers knew me well. Indeed, there were plenty of good memories. Once, a psychotic woman lost all touch with reality in the store and stripped naked, screaming. She appeared to be about 300 pounds, and her yelling could be heard throughout the whole building. Except for me, of course.

While everyone could hear her coming and got out of the way as they waited for the police to come, she rumbled straight to the aisle where I was working. The entire crew from my department peeked around the end shelf, barely able to contain their laughter. I was quietly marking up boxes of cigars, oblivious to this naked version of Godzilla screaming right at my face. When I finally looked up and saw what stood before me, I did what must have been the double-take of the century. Completely disoriented, I dropped the cigars and slinked off to the nearest corner in a catatonic state of shock. The guys were laughing hysterically as it began to hit me that yes, there really was a large naked woman yelling at me. The police arrived shortly afterwards, and order was restored quickly. Sure, the whole thing was over in a few minutes, but the guys would be reminding me about my new girlfriend for *years.*

Another incident I recall at the supermarket was the time I was working the night shift. It was boring; not many people were around, and nothing ever happened. On one typically dull evening, I took a much-needed coffee break and noticed that a couple of other employees were acting strangely. One of them was actually shaking as she sipped from her cup. She looked kind of bugged out, like she had jumped out of her skin. You'd think that the place just got robbed or something.

As it turned out, the place *was* robbed. Cashiers, front-desk employees and a customer or two were all lying on the floor, while a pair of gunmen emptied the registers. Meanwhile, I was nonchalantly stocking shelves no more than two aisles away from all the mayhem. Had I just turned around the corner of the aisle, I would have been peeing myself instead of moping about how boring it was.

As exciting as it was to be working with nude women and masked gunmen, there was still the gnawing sense that something was missing. I didn't know it yet, but a caring woman named Linda Baine certainly did. She was the new Coordinator of Residence Education at the Pennsylvania School for the Deaf, running the dormitory and the afterschool program. Sometime in December 1987, a dorm supervisor had left and Linda needed to find a replacement over the Christmas break. She had ten days to find someone. By chance, she had gone out to a staff get-together that my mother also happened to be attending. Somehow my name came up in conversation, and Linda suddenly remembered me from a time she met me briefly once before. A few years ago, I had been asked by PSD to be a guest speaker on a panel involving deaf people with different educational backgrounds, as a number of people were curious about what it was like for me to be the only deaf student at GFS. As fate would have it, Linda was working as an interpreter at that event. Fast-forward to 1987, and here she was remembering me at some staff party. She immediately figured out I would be the perfect candidate for the job opening as Resident Advisor and afterschool program basketball/baseball coach. She knew that not only would the kids learn from me, but I would learn from them as well. I still had a poor deaf identity at the time, and Linda knew just what I needed.

Linda went out of her way to come shopping at my supermarket, just to get a chance to talk to me. She pulled me aside one day while I was packing the shelves as usual. She told me how working at PSD would be a good opportunity for me and spilled out all the details. The job required supervising fourteen kids in a dorm, as well as planning activities and occasional trips for them. In addition to that, there would be the aforementioned coaching responsibilities for the afterschool program. I would coach sports from 2:30 to 4:00, then after that I would head to the dorm and work there until 11:00pm. The pay was terrible, yes, but it included free room and board. I would get my own room on the boys' floor and be able to live there throughout the whole school year, even on weekends when the dorm kids went home. I could just about hear my party-hardy friends cheering in the background at this thought.

As much as this decision should have been a no-brainer, I struggled with it for a while. It represented a massive change in the comfortable, safe, boring life I was leading. Of the fourteen kids I would be responsible for, only a small number of them were staying in the dorm because they lived too far for daily transportation. The rest were in there because certain social workers had recommended such an arrangement; these kids had such difficult lives at home, that it was agreed a dorm would offer a more safe, accessible environment conductive to learning. This job was no piece of cake, it was going to be a big challenge and I knew it. On top of that, the supermarket was paying me very good money. But then again, the supermarket wasn't providing me with a place of my own.

As I continued wrestling with this decision, Linda could have blown me off while I stalled in the face of the fast-approaching deadline. Instead, she actually came to visit me at work two more times, to further explain why this job would not only be a great experience, but also an opportunity for tremendous personal growth. From a financial standpoint, I was ready to turn her down, seeing how I was due for yet another raise in just a few months. Yet something gnawed at me inside, and Linda did a great job selling me on the virtues of PSD. Finally, with no more than a day or two left on the deadline, I called Linda and told her I accepted.

Working at PSD was an entirely new experience for me. Up until that point, my entire existence had pretty much consisted of being the only deaf guy at school, at work, or on the baseball field. I was always following orders or whatever everyone else was doing. It was time to stop being a follower and start being a leader. For the first time in my life, I had a considerable number of kids looking up to me. I didn't always have the answers, but Linda always had faith in me, offering support and advice whenever necessary. As with Deborah, my interpreter at GFS, I was once again under the wing of a hearing person teaching me how to be Deaf. At times, it was hard for me to admit that a hearing person could be so much more fluent than I was at ASL (as was the case with both Deb and Linda), but I knew I was gaining valuable insight.

On one occasion, Linda gave me a paper with an important announcement related to PSD; it was my responsibility to relay this information to the kids I supervised. Linda reviewed the memo with me and asked if I was confident I could explain everything to the kids myself.

"Oh, sure," I signed to her. "I'll run it by them, signing it over step by step. If the kids don't understand, I'll 'drop' my signing to ASL and repeat it."

"Whoa, wait a minute," Linda intervened. "You mean you will *adjust*, or *switch*, to ASL." I had signed "drop" like ASL was one notch below the signed English I tended to use; Linda had correctly pointed out that neither was better than the other. Both English and ASL are languages in their own right. Most deaf kids respond to and learn better from ASL, Linda explained. It would be quite a few years later, when I attended grad school, before I fully understood why this was so. Nonetheless, Linda had succeeded in converting me: I began to try communicating exclusively through ASL from there on. Thus began the rebirth of a true Deaf (capital "D" emphasized) man. Or, as the saying goes in ASL, "true-business, Deaf."

Just about everything at PSD was new to me. Not only was I learning more about deafness and further developing my sign language skills, but I was also learning more about myself. I discovered that during the morning and early afternoon hours, the recreation room of the dorm doubled as the playroom for an Early Intervention program. As previously explained, deaf children of hearing parents are usually behind in overall linguistic and cognitive development due to lack of effective communication; this is where they work at closing the gap.

Again, the ages 0–5 are a crucial window for children to pick up language. If sufficient communication has not occurred during these years, the child begins school having to play catch-up. This gap is a key reason why many deaf adults today can barely read at the fourth grade level. Some deaf people, like my parents, also blame the old oral schools... they point out that if they had received sign language instruction in their day, they could have learned so much more.

In the Early Intervention program, I noticed that there was a comprehensive plan designed to facilitate the deaf child's social, emotional, intellectual and linguistic development. Parents would come in with their deaf toddlers, and drop them off in a play area where they got to interact with other deaf children (in addition to this, PSD staff also offers home-based services as well). They were supervised all the while by staff fluent in ASL, who led fun activities designed to develop communication skills. Meanwhile, the parents would go upstairs and work with other PSD staff, who would educate them on ways to accelerate their children's development. Sign language classes are offered, and are of course a vital part of the program.

Although I could understand the overall philosophy of the Early Intervention program, its importance never really struck me until several years later, when a Deaf couple I know began raising their three Deaf children. My friends, George and Val Oshman, communicate with their kids exclusively through ASL. Their oldest child, Travis, completely won me over on the virtues of ASL when he was only four years of age. There are two incidents that will be permanently tattooed to my brain, stored for future reference should I ever have deaf children.

The first such incident occurred when Travis' mom had to fly to Chicago to be with a relative who had fallen ill. Everyone at PSD was enamored when they saw four-year old Travis, in fluent ASL, explaining to his teachers that his mom specifically flew to Chicago to help take care of the sick relative in question. His signing skills and ability to effectively communicate *exactly* what was happening (including all of the relevant who, what, when, where and why's) was way advanced for a deaf child his age. Most other deaf children at that age, who come from hearing families that do not sign, would only have been able to say something like "Mom fly, gone" or just "Mom gone..." and not have been able to elaborate any further. To see Travis saying "Mom flew to Chicago because..." truly demonstrated the benefits of early exposure to ASL.

The second example with Travis is hilarious, but nonetheless shows the virtues of effective sign communication with deaf children. It so happened that one day, George and Val were chagrined to discover that their dog had somehow got out of the yard and ran off. In their endeavor to find the dog (which, fortunately, was successful), they made "Lost Dog" posters to distribute around the neighborhood. Val went out to staple some of the posters on local telephone poles, accompanied by four-year old Travis. Ever curious, he asked his mom why they were posting up pictures of their dog. In ASL, Val explained that if someone in the neighborhood saw the dog, they would recognize it from the posters and call home. Travis indicated he understood how it worked, and proceeded to help his mom put up more posters. On one telephone pole, there was also a poster of a man running for office. Travis tugged at his mom's shirt, pointed at the picture of the political candidate, and asked,

"Is his mom upset because he's lost, too?"

Val cracked up and explained that the politician's poster was for an entirely different reason.

Granted, Travis made a cute assumption with his four-year old logic. It was amusing how he made this connection between the dog and the politician, but it was also significant in showing his level of cognitive development. He might have jumped to the wrong conclusion, but that was irrelevant. The important thing was, he was *thinking*. He was putting two and two together in the cute way that only a four-year old can. He was developing his logic and reasoning skills. Had his parents not been able to communicate effectively with him from day one in a language that is fully accessible to him, he might not have even come close to the level of thinking and communicating where he is today. Instead of the ever-painful "nevermind" or "I'll tell you later" that many deaf children get from their parents, Travis gets all of the input any growing child so rightfully deserves.

By taking note of Travis' experiences, you can see why PSD's Early Intervention program (as well as numerous others throughout the country) advocates early exposure to and use of ASL. By encouraging use of ASL and an understanding of deafness, the Early Intervention program helps parents close the communication gap with their deaf children so that they are better equipped to deal with the upcoming school years. Most important of all, it improves the relationship between parents and their deaf children.

If it appears that I'm beginning to get a bit preachy about ASL, please excuse me. I admit that it's not the easy-as-ABC solution I might have made it appear to be. I have also, through my observation and brief interaction with the Early Intervention program, come to understand how hard it can be on parents to have to deal with deafness. It is not easy at all. It's not as simple as "oh, you just need to take courses in ASL, you'll be fine." It's a lot more complicated than that. Parents have more needs than just learning ASL; they have a number of difficult issues they must work through. Some or all may have lingering feelings of shock, denial, anger, and even guilt left over from the initial diagnosis of their child's deafness. One parent admitted feeling embarrassed when her child signed in public, and consequently felt guilty; did she not have a moral obligation to love her child unconditionally, instead of worrying about what others thought? Through the support of other parents in the program, she found that she was not alone in having those and many other thoughts and feelings. Consequently, she was able to deal with them better.

Conversely, through the Early Intervention program, I found out that I was not alone, either. I only worked with the Early Intervention staff once or twice, when they asked me to share my experiences with parents, but I learned so much from it. For the first time, I could see deafness through my hearing grandparents' eyes. I could never understand what the big deal was the way they reacted (or over-reacted) to my deafness. In talking with parents in the Early Intervention program, I finally got a sense of what my grandparents went through... and could better understand their pain and difficulty in accepting my deafness.

One parent of a prelingually deaf child caught me using my voice (which is not perfect, but pretty comprehensible), and wanted to know nothing but how her own child could develop his voice similarly. It was hard explaining to her (and getting her to accept) that I had lost my hearing *after* acquiring speech skills, and that communication in ASL was probably more desirable for her child. Seeing the parents' initial denial, however, helped me better understand the denial I saw in my own family. Not only did I understand now, but also I could accept it and even laugh about it.

In fact, shortly before I quit my supermarket job for good (I initially made an ill-advised attempt at moonlighting before switching solely to PSD), there was this one time a relative came in the store. She approached Jim, a co-worker and good friend of mine, asking him where she could find me. The thing was, there were two people named Mark working there, so Jim tried to clarify by asking,

"The Mark in the produce section, or the deaf Mark?" The relative in question gasped and gave him a shocked look. When she composed herself, she retorted:

"He's not deaf!" Jim scratched his head, backed off, and told her to wait a second. He came into the back room where I was on break.

"Uh, Mark..." he began. "I have good news and bad news. The good news is, you're not deaf anymore... congratulations. The bad news is, one of your relatives is out there and boy, is she pissed off!"

Rather than getting into a family argument, I just smiled and went out there. I just greeted the relative, and laughed about the whole thing with Jim later on. Instead of being angry, I actually understood the denial behind the whole incident. It was nothing personal, no insult. I would let the relative deal with it, and later, when she was ready, she would accept my deafness and even make an effort to learn sign language.

Speaking of sign language, I must admit that however desirable, you can't just learn ASL overnight. It takes time and commitment. Some people have trouble picking up a knack for ASL; my grandfather, for example, was so uncoordinated in his signing skills that anytime he tried to sign the letter "D," he inadvertently wound up giving me the finger.

Regardless of whether or not anyone is a natural at picking up sign language, it is certainly worth the effort if you have deaf children. They deserve to be in an environment where they are comfortable and able to understand and enjoy all that is being said around them. Even if your signing skills are marginal at best, your deaf child will become accustomed to your "accent" of signing and be grateful that you thought so much of him or her to take the effort to learn. When I got the job at PSD, it felt so good to be able to relax and just soak up all of the information that came through so clearly in sign language.

Some parents of deaf children choose to take a different, more radical approach: cochlear implants. This involves surgically implanting an electrode array in the cochlea and a receiver/stimulator in the vicinity of the mastoid bone behind the ear. When combined with an outer microphone that can be worn externally behind the ear, this system works as a bypass, carrying sound around damaged inner ear nerves that do not function properly. This is not a bona fide cure for deafness, however. There have been varying results and some limited benefits (such as awareness of environmental sounds, some ability to recognize speech and some improved speechreading), but there has never been a case of Joe Deaf going under the knife and coming out of it Joe Hearing. It is not the miracle some people try to make it appear to be.

I'm sorry for being so obviously biased in my opinion, but I don't think the cochlear implant is an ideal option for deaf children. Granted, the implant is not a total flop; there are some cases where it has significantly improved the hearing in those who underwent the surgical procedure. I personally know some late-deafened adults who opted for the implant. One of them seems happy with it. He signs fluently when he's with deaf people, and interacts well with hearing people... he makes the best of both worlds. As an adult, he weighed the positives and negatives of the whole procedure, and made a decision for himself.

However, I like to look at all perspectives and all experiences, and there are many which vary. For example, there's the guy who got the implant and went through an excruciating experience. The day after his surgery, he forgot that the Eustachian tube runs from the ear to the nasal area, and he made an ill-advised attempt at blowing his nose. He blew out his sutures, and the resulting complications were horrendous. Although he recovered from that fiasco, he said the implant was "disorienting" and no longer uses it.

To complete the continuum of differing perspectives on the implant, there is a third person I personally know who has one. He describes it as "alright", but sometimes wishes he simply stuck with wearing his hearing aids. Again, as with the other adults, it was his decision and he's living with it.

The key word here, however, is "adult." An adult can make the decision for him or herself to get an implant if he/she really wants one. If any adults want some electronic equipment surgically implanted in their heads, that's their prerogative. No one has any business telling them not to do it. I've had various adults e-mail me and tell me they're happy with their implants, and I'm happy for them. Likewise, I've received e-mails from adults who regret getting implanted. It all balances out and I neither condemn nor object to what they do. They are adults, and what they do with their lives is none of my business.

For deaf children, however, I have certain reservations. When I look at all the risks involved (there are quite a few, believe me) and all of the hassles that come with the implant even if all goes well, I just don't think its worth it to subject young children to this kind of drastic procedure. I have heard too many stories about deaf high school and college students who have the implant, but never hook it up... they only got it because their parents wanted them to.

Maybe it's just me... in all honesty, I admit I am biased against "fixing" deaf children. After being operated on four times to have tubes put in my ears, after all the trips to ear, nose and throat specialists, being fitted for hearing aids, going through countless tests, going through speech therapy... I'd just about *had* it with all attempts at fixing me before I even reached high school age. Although I never really spoke up when I was real young... deep down inside, I always had this strong desire for people to stop poking around my ears. I wanted them to stop trying to fix me like I was some kind of defective machinery, and to just accept me for who I am.

All of this fussing over my ears just made me want to crawl under a rock and hide. I don't know which was worse: the incessant tinkering around with my ears, or the unrealistic expectations that came with it. I was being set up for failure, because I just couldn't hear no matter how bad everyone wanted me to. So I can tell you right now that if the cochlear implant were available when I was a young kid, they would have had to drag me kicking and screaming into the operating room.

In fact, once it became available, a number of people in my family tried to talk me into getting the implant. The worst argument in favor of this came from a relative who said,

"...but Mark, you're so smart, you *can* learn how to hear."

I sighed in exasperation. The implied correlation between intelligence and deafness left me scratching my head. Later on, I would learn that this was a common mistake; there are many who erroneously assume that deaf people who have residual hearing and speech ability are smarter than those who do not. With a similar mindset, my own family apparently thought that it was my level of intelligence, not my degree of hearing loss, that made me a viable candidate for the cochlear implant. Interesting. Regardless, I really wish people would just accept the package I was born with, instead of incessantly searching for ways to change it.

Some people may feel that my objectivity leaves much to be desired in this area, so I recommend that you do your own research and come to your own conclusions. Any literature that addresses the implant, pro or con, will do just fine. Read over all of the positives and negatives, and ask yourself if you think it's really fair to subject a young child to the whole procedure. Think about the surgery, the related risks, follow-up appointments with specialists, the required (and intensive) auditory/speech training, all with no guarantee of success. Compare that to simply enrolling in a sign language class.

Now tell me if you still like the idea of putting a cochlear implant in a young child who's still struggling to find his or her real identity in the world. I'm sorry, but I give a big "no thank you" to the implant. As I found in my new environment at PSD, sign language gave me an opportunity to be one hundred percent receptive to all that went on around me. No amount of speech therapy or medical intervention could ever come close to providing me with that kind of satisfaction.

But you know what? It's never that simple. When the original version of *Deaf Again* came out in 1997, I trashed the cochlear implant (with much satisfaction) and left it at that. And no, my ranting and raving did not change the world. Deaf kids are still getting implanted, more so than ever before. It has even been predicted that in the near future, it won't be unusual to see fifty percent of the kids in any deaf program having a cochlear implant.

And I have found myself working in close proximity with many of these kids... and their parents. The cochlear implant is no longer somewhere *out there*, it is now in my own backyard. Most parents are no longer looking at the cochlear implant as a magic cure-all, they are just looking at it as another option that may or may not improve their child's hearing. They are also under pressure to make a difficult decision, spurred on by doctors and research which give the impression that the earlier a child is implanted, the better. I do recognize they are trying to take advantage of every option they can. Not only do many of these parents have their children implanted, but they also pursue other avenues, including ASL and Deaf culture.

Imagine the awkwardness when I was working closely with three parents who were trying to implement a sign language program in their children's school district... and two of those parents had kids with cochlear implants. How do you think they felt, after the fact, when they got their hands on this book? The damage had been done, and I got no pleasure out of making my point. Remember my grandfather's famous quote, "I don't want to prove, with a broken arm, that I had the right of way?" Sometimes I feel like I don't want to prove, by breaking several hearts, that my cochlear implant opinions are justified.

Generally, I feel my message is entirely appropriate, as people can definitely benefit from seeing a Deaf person's point of view (hey, our opinion counts, doesn't it?). Yet there are also times when I feel a twinge of guilt, as I can also put myself in a parent's shoes and understand the overwhelming, difficult choices they have to make. It's not easy at all, but if people ask, then I try my best to show a Deaf perspective as tactfully as possible.

Well… truthfully, my personal opinion hasn't really changed. I'm not crazy about *any* surgery, to be honest. But this time around, I do advocate for more tolerance and understanding. Many hearing parents are getting their kids implanted, and many of those kids are someday going join the Deaf community. It is our responsibility to welcome them. If we spend too much time criticizing their decisions instead of just educating them about the positive aspects of the Deaf community, we will push them away… and it will be our loss.

No, the Cochlear Corporation of America did not bribe me to soften my stance. What actually happened was I went out and got a kid of my own (gory details to follow in an upcoming chapter). After becoming a father, I noticed that every idiot and his brother was bombarding me with advice on how to raise my kid. And now I completely understand how hearing parents feel when Deaf people like myself are too outspoken against their choices… choices that are none of my business.

Granted, getting a job at PSD was a very positive experience for me. Slowly, in the two years I worked there as Resident Advisor, I began to grow a strong sense of Deaf identity. Being with other Deaf people and hearing people who signed gave me an opportunity to be completely involved, in a more enriching way than I was used to in the past. Rather than being mostly an observer, I was usually an active participant, as other staff valued my input and opinions. Although I still needed to refine my signing skills somewhat, I felt like an equal amongst them. I enjoyed working with the kids in the dorm, who looked up to me. Big deal, some people might say, as I was just a dorm counselor. But it was the first time I could recall anyone ever looking up to me. In all my years of succeeding in the tough academic environment at GFS, I had never once considered myself to be a leader (nor did I ever imagine I had the potential to be one). At PSD, this was my first taste.

Although the kids looked up to me, deep down I was also looking up to them. Right before my very eyes, they were developing social and leadership skills I never had when I was in school. Everyone interacted as an equal, and it was reflected in their self-esteem and confidence; anytime a kid disagreed with something, he or she said so. Anytime a kid felt something could be done better, he or she spoke up, and offered another point of view or idea. When I was in school, I didn't dare rock the boat... I was too busy playing catch-up, too busy trying to fit in with hearing people. With my hearing family, with my hearing classmates, and in my relationship with a hearing girlfriend, I always felt I had to be super-nice and super-perfect to be accepted. There's nothing wrong with being a nice guy or trying to be the best you can be, but when it comes to doing so at the expense of your true inner feelings and desires, then it's no good. That's called living a lie.

For example, earlier I mentioned that with my hearing girlfriend Karen, I would willingly go to movies with her, pretending to enjoy them because I didn't want her to feel bad for me. I wanted to be accepted, to be seen as a normal guy who could do anything with her. At PSD, I saw students many years younger than me saying,

"Nah, I don't like to go to the movies, they're not captioned. I'd rather wait for the video to come out, then watch it captioned on my VCR with a decoder."

These kids were being genuine, living in the present moment and accepting fully who they were and what they felt. There was nothing wrong with being deaf, nothing wrong with waiting for captioned videos to come out. They knew it, I didn't. These kids were wise beyond their years, and wiser than I ever had been. Biologically speaking, I may have been 22 years of age at that time, but the real me, the fully-actualized Deaf Mark Drolsbaugh, was only about one or two years old.

Chapter 7

It was early March 1988. On one brisk afternoon, I had enjoyed a vibrant morning workout at Tae Kwon Do class, then got set to go to work at PSD. It was a good day, and I felt particularly refreshed. I was feeling quite energetic, more so than usual. Arriving early at PSD, I did some homework for a class I was attending at Temple University. I was taking a few courses part-time, pulling in A's and B's. Much better than the time I was on academic probation, but college was still a somewhat hollow experience for me. I was missing out somehow.

On this day, however, even a dreary homework assignment couldn't get me down. I finished quickly and bounced down the stairs of the dorm, ready for another day on the job. Linda was already in the hallway on the first floor, and she greeted me with some unbelievable news.

"Did you hear about Gallaudet? The students are on strike." I did a double-take. I must have misunderstood.

"What?" I asked. "The teachers went on strike? What for?"

"No, the *students* went on strike. There was an election for President of Gallaudet University, and two of the three finalists were Deaf. The hearing person won, and now the students have shut down the university and are demanding a Deaf president."

Whoa. This was something else. This was big, this was history. This was an awakening, as you could feel the surge in Deaf pride throughout the world. That whole week, March 6 to March 13, had everyone's attention.

Up until that point, I had never really given much thought to Gallaudet, which is located in Washington, D.C. Even though I heard about it, I never fully considered going there. Back in 1984, I had chosen Temple, so that I could stay in the Philadelphia area and be close to my girlfriend. Bad move, I know. But that was then and this was now, and now Gallaudet had my undivided attention. It had everyone's undivided attention. Students and staff at PSD posted banners in support of the Gallaudet students' quest (as did many deaf schools all over the world), and the whole Deaf community was abuzz.

It didn't take long for the events at Gallaudet to cause a stir in the hearing world, either. This protest, which came to be called Deaf President Now, featured students, alumni, countless supporters and many leaders of the Deaf community. Not only were the gates to Gallaudet effectively blockaded, but also there was an emotional march to the Capitol. First there was local media coverage, then it went national. Greg Hlibok, one of the student leaders behind the protest, was interviewed on ABC's *Nightline* for the whole world to see. Jesse Jackson offered his support to the Deaf community. And so on and so on... this thing was big.

The solidarity felt among the Deaf community was unbelievable. I could feel it in Philadelphia, and I knew there were Deaf people who could feel it in Bora Bora. Dr. Elizabeth Zinser, the hearing President-elect of Gallaudet University, certainly felt it. She acknowledged what was happening around her and resigned her post.

Finally, on March 13, 1988, it was announced that Dr. I. King Jordan, a long-time Deaf faculty member at Gallaudet, had been selected as the new President of Gallaudet University. The entire campus erupted in celebration, as did the Deaf community all over the world. For an in-depth, historical account of everything that led *u*p to the Deaf President Now movement, I highly recommend Dr. Jack Gannon's book, T*he Week the World Heard Gallaudet.* As a Deaf individual, I consider this event to be one of the most significant parts of my heritage. Chalk this up as something to repeatedly tell the grandkids, with a deep sense of Deaf pride.

Shortly after the Deaf President Now movement, there would be some changes in PSD that would affect me directly. Sometime in the following year, it was decided that the PSD dorm would have to close. The number of residential students had dwindled from fourteen to eight, a far cry from the days of residential life at the old PSD, which used to be located in nearby Mt. Airy. By 1983, the rubella surge of deaf students had significantly subsided, so that the number of incoming deaf students had predictably declined. On top of that, political interpretation of PL 94-142 and its proposed "least restrictive environment" ideology resulted in a number of good students being pulled from PSD and placed into mainstream schools, whether they or their parents wanted it or not.

Today, many residential schools face similar issues. Instead of being ideal places for advanced education, several are becoming dumping grounds for deaf kids who couldn't succeed in the mainstream schools. By the time they finally transfer to deaf schools, they are way behind. My fear is that many people will look at deaf schools and surmise that they must be lacking, and perhaps make the same assumptions about the use of ASL in the classroom. I myself was once guilty of such an assumption (we'll get to that part later). The truth is many deaf schools face the formidable challenge of having to fill up their classes with kids no one else could handle.

Getting back to the bottom line, it turned out that the decline in rubella babies and the advent of PL 94-142 affected PSD's student population so much, that it was no longer economically feasible to run a K-12 school on what was a large campus. In 1984, PSD made the move to its current Germantown location, where it would no longer run a high school curriculum. Instead, PSD now offers an academic program for students ages 3-15 (along with Early Intervention services for ages 0-3). Since those big changes in the mid-eighties, PSD has bounced back quite strongly, becoming a big part of the Germantown community.

By 1989, however, there was one more big change looming on the horizon, and that was the closing of the dorm. Since there were only eight residential students left (out of about 175 students overall), it didn't make sense to run an entire residential program. Instead, it would make more sense to use the dorm building in such a manner that it could serve much more than just eight people. The dorm would close, and in its place would be the new Center for Community and Professional Services. CCPS would have a public relations office and a community outreach program which included sign language classes, adult literacy classes, social services for the Deaf community, an AIDS education program, and of course a continuation of the successful Early Intervention program. Closing the dorm was not a step backward, but instead a step forward which made better use of the space available.

This step forward, however, meant that my days as a Resident Advisor were numbered. Not that PSD was going to leave me hanging in the cold, however. Headmaster Joseph Fischgrund had seen to it that all residential staff were offered regular day jobs for the fall of 1989. For me, however, the changes in store meant it was time to move on. It was either accept a job as a teacher aide (the only position I was qualified for), or transfer from Temple to Gallaudet University. Linda had often encouraged me to someday go there when the time was right, and at this juncture, the time was now.

In August of 1989, I did what I probably should have done years ago, packing my bags and heading to Gallaudet University. For the first time in my life, I would be a student in a place where deaf peers surrounded me. I had waited long enough for an experience like this, and what awaited me was one of the most magical periods of my life.

During the two-week New Student Orientation program prior to the start of fall classes, I made a lot of friends immediately, something I'd never done in any other educational setting. In between getting to know each other and touring Washington D.C., there were placement exams and other stuff that would determine what level of classes we would be taking in certain subjects. Although NSO had many practical purposes, the best one was that it enabled us to establish a strong base of friends whom we could lean on for support for the rest of our college years.

Academically, once school started in September, I found myself with a mixed bag. On one hand, the results of my English evaluation test during NSO waived me from general English requirements; instead of the required two years of English classes (which students had to take upon the passing or waiving of a remedial English 50 course), I could take one year of Honors English and be done with it. On the other hand, the math test I took during NSO indicated that I had to take a remedial Algebra II class, which ticked me off. I had taken calculus during my senior year at GFS, and for that reason chose not to take it again at Temple University. Instead, I took a higher-level math course that was related to the principles of accounting and business. Gallaudet, however, required that I specifically have calculus on a college transcript in order to be waived from all math requirements.

I tried explaining my circumstances, but to no avail. I had to take the math proficiency test, and I couldn't remember most of the complex formulas and applications I had learned more than five years ago. Mathematically speaking, I was a dinosaur. I barely managed to score high enough to waive the Algebra I and Geometry requirements, but found myself stuck having to take Algebra II... a course I had taken midway through high school at GFS.

Even worse, I was horrified to find that upon review of my transcript, the admissions office had informed me that it could not accept about thirty of my credits from Temple University. A number of courses at Temple were not offered at Gallaudet, so I couldn't get credit for them. I was livid. I had put in a lot of effort to get through what was approximately two and a half years of academic work, and now Gallaudet was telling me that one of those years was being thrown away.

By this point, as quickly as I decided to enroll at Gallaudet University, I decided to withdraw. Maybe I did have somewhat of a chip on my shoulder, somewhat of a snobbish attitude. What with my academic background at GFS and an English level which blew away those of several other students, I egotistically assumed that I was one step ahead of everyone else. If anything, I figured I should have had one year waived from my requirements, not eliminated from my transcript.

Fortunately, a friend I met during NSO, Vijay Advani, talked me out of leaving Gallaudet at the last minute. Yes, he acknowledged, there was going to be some drudgery in dealing with The System, which could be insultingly paternalistic at times. On the other hand, Vijay pointed out all of the things I had missed out on as a mainstreamed student in high school. There were plenty of positive experiences, both social and academic, which were awaiting me. Wasn't NSO one of the most enjoyable times of my life? Couldn't I just taste the excitement of living in a different world, one that was 100 percent accessible to me?

Vijay was right. I wasn't going anywhere. Besides, he pointed out, I needed to learn both social and survival skills... such as how to be assertive when necessary. I needed to learn how to take charge of my life. In the hearing world, I had grown accustomed to not always knowing what was going on... and thus I tended to give up by just accepting whatever cards were dealt to me. It was time, Vijay emphasized, that I stood up for myself. He had a point. I went straight to the admissions office and filed an appeal for further review of my transcript. I wound up getting fifteen of my credits back. For me, it was a great victory. It was nice to fight for myself instead of watching hearing family or friends do it for me.

As fate would have it, my very first class as a Gallaudet student was going to be that remedial Algebra II class I was so upset about. I arrived early for the eight a.m. class, grumbling how I felt like I was back in high school instead of in a reputable university. My disgust, however, immediately switched to delight as the teacher walked in and introduced herself. She was a Deaf woman, and she was signing in her native ASL. For me, this was history... my first ever Deaf teacher. Unbelievable! Everywhere I looked, I could understand clearly what was being said, at the very moment it was being said. Whenever the teacher or the students signed, information was there for me to instantly comprehend, as plain as day. With an interpreter in high school, I was always a few seconds behind. Not anymore! Finally I felt like I was really there, experiencing everything as it happened. I wasn't living in a fishbowl anymore. I noticed that I was incredibly relaxed, a big difference compared to how I was always on edge in high school. Wonder of wonders... was I actually *enjoying* a class?

Yes, I was. My teacher's ASL was too good to be true, it was blowing me away. Although I had accomplished a lot in math at both GFS and Temple, it took a lot of hard work and frustration at every level. For the first time anywhere, I was not struggling to grasp anything. The instructor's ASL was so smooth and clear that I could literally see the concepts and comprehend them right away. Her hands, utilizing the space around her, deftly gave the impression of factors dividing in the air. ASL, as I could see very well here, happens to be very spatial and conceptual, and I had much to benefit from this exposure. Yes, I had qualified interpreters in high school and college, but they weren't math teachers themselves. I had to follow them following spoken instructions, plus I had to glance back and forth between them and the blackboard. The bits and pieces that I missed were apparently more important than I had realized, and I had difficulty grasping a number of concepts. With the use of ASL, however, concepts were smacking me right in the face in a way that's hard to describe. I couldn't miss.

As I was contemplating on how my first exposure to ASL in the classroom environment had a big impact on me, I couldn't help thinking of a book I once read, Alan Watts' *Cloud-Hidden, Whereabouts Unknown*. Watts was ruminating on the beauty of Chinese writing in 1970 when he said:

"...I have always been in love with Chinese writing. Each character, or ideogram, is an abstract picture of some feature of the process of nature— that is, of the Tao, the Way or Course of the universe. When translated very literally into English, Chinese reads like a telegram. 'Tao

can Tao not eternal Tao,' or 'Way can speak-about not eternal Way.' In contrast with English, and particularly German or Japanese, Chinese is the fastest and shortest way of saying things, both in speech and in writing. If, as seems possible, Mao Tse-Tung's people switch to an alphabetic form of writing, they will be at a great disadvantage, for, as their own proverb says, 'One picture is worth a thousand words.'"

When I read the above statement in Watts' book, I realized that he very well could have been describing the beauty of ASL: one sign is worth a thousand words. After my experiences with ASL at PSD, which then culminated at Gallaudet, I am one of the staunchest advocates for ASL in the classroom. It's a beautiful thing.

Not every teacher, however, was as fluent in ASL as the students might have liked. If I had to rank the teachers based on signing skill, I would use a continuum that ran from beginner to intermediate to advanced to native ASL. My estimate is that most of the teachers fall in between intermediate and advanced. A small number sign terribly, and a small number sign native-like ASL. If you got a lousy-signing teacher, tough luck... and if you got a Deaf teacher who signed fluent ASL (like my aforementioned math teacher), you hit the jackpot.

To me, however, a teacher's signing ability didn't really matter that much, so long as it wasn't horrendous. Yes, I preferred ASL, but it didn't bother me the least if I had a hearing teacher with a tendency to use SEE (Signed Exact English). SEE doesn't hold a candle to ASL in terms of convenience and practicality, but I could tolerate it. After all those years in hearing schools with no interpreter, *any* teacher who signed, no matter how awkwardly, was a blessing. Even if a teacher's signing skill was marginal at best, I still preferred it to having a skilled interpreter in a hearing school. With a teacher who signs, I could let my eyes wander all over; I could follow the teacher, then glance to the students, and so on. With an interpreter, you have to just sit there, with your eyes glued to that same limited space all day. It's exhausting on the eyes. Give me a signing teacher any day, even if she's using the Rochester method. The Gallaudet faculty, regardless of signing level, was an incredibly liberating thrill for me.

Despite my exuberance over the fact that all of my teachers signed, there were a number of students who complained about lack of teachers who used bona fide ASL. Most of these students were prelingually deaf and/or native ASL users themselves. I was intrigued by their argument that every teacher should be using ASL, because it wasn't that much of a big deal to me. Then I realized that I had an unfair advantage; my residual hearing was good enough so that I could use a combination of hearing and lip-reading, which were supported by whatever signing skills a teacher had. For example, I could hear a teacher's voice, but not comprehend everything she was saying. But when she signed, that would fill in the blanks.

Likewise, if the same teacher signed something incorrectly, my ability to hear her voice and read her lips would compensate for the incorrect sign. Many prelingually deaf students do not have this ability. With this in mind, I decided to try an experiment. I would zero in on the teacher's hands, completely ignoring her voice and her lips. I was shocked to find that in many cases, I became completely lost. It often looked like the teacher was signing in broken sentences, and sometimes, jumping completely off the point. It was disorienting. Later on, I would try this same experiment in a number of deaf residential schools, with the same results. Only when a teacher signed in true ASL was I able to fully comprehend what was being said. So again... for prelingually deaf students, I cannot emphasize enough the value of true ASL in the classroom.

Eventually, a student organization at Gallaudet took it upon themselves to publish an underground guidebook that rated the teachers based on their signing competence and overall content of classroom work. It was a brutally honest guidebook. The administration was not too pleased, and a number of teachers were livid. But it helped. I personally took advantage of it myself. When it came to taking courses that were related to my weakest areas, such as science and technology, I tried my best to make sure I got into a class where the teacher used ASL. Technical idiot that I am, I never would have received a B+ in the Television, Film and Photography course if it weren't for the Deaf teacher who signed in ASL. That's just the way it is.

After the initial thrill of being in a Deaf university, things eventually settled down a bit. It took a while for me to take off my rose-colored glasses because I was in awe of the legacy of Gallaudet. This was, after all, the highly publicized "only university in the world for the deaf." At the time I transferred, Gallaudet was given a high rating by *U.S. News and World Report,* which conducted a poll on the best colleges and universities in the United States. Based on the results of their survey, Gallaudet was declared the best liberal arts college in the East. Add that to the whole brouhaha over the Deaf President Now movement, and it's no wonder I felt like I was in the Deaf Mecca of the world.

Social life at Gallaudet, not surprisingly, was incredible. I estimate that in about one or two semesters at Gallaudet, I made more friends than I did in an entire lifetime of attending hearing schools in Philadelphia. I was in Deaf heaven.

Being in the world's largest melting pot for deaf people was not without its ramifications, however. There is a very wide continuum of deaf people with varying communication skills and backgrounds. There are Deaf children of Deaf parents who are fluent in ASL and have a strong language base. There are Deaf children of hearing parents who took every effort to learn ASL and exposed their kids to it. There are deaf children of hearing parents who use SEE (Signing Exact English) to communicate. There are deaf children of hearing parents who have no knowledge or interest in any kind of sign language whatsoever. There are deaf children of hearing parents who strictly enforce the oral method. Then there are those who are hard of hearing and late-deafened, some them coming to Gallaudet with no sign language ability at all.

If that isn't diverse enough, now try to factor in the varying educational backgrounds of all of these deaf people. There are residential schools for the deaf, day schools for the deaf, mainstream programs in hearing schools, and then there are oral schools where signing is not encouraged. Some deaf children, like I did, just attend hearing schools with or without an interpreter and find a way to get by. Not only is the use (or non-use) of sign language an issue here, but we also have to keep in mind the quality of the curricula itself. Some deaf programs are good, some are lacking. The same goes for mainstream programs. Some may be good in terms of academic content, but are insufficient nonetheless because of differing communication methodologies leaving some deaf students completely lost. Also, there are a considerable number of international students who come from countries where programs and services for the deaf are unheard of. And so on, and so on.

Now take all of these varying types of deaf people with such diverse social and educational backgrounds, and throw them into the only university in the world for the deaf. What do you have? Several professors scratching their heads wondering how to accommodate everyone.

Unfortunately, it becomes an awkward situation. What happens is that some teachers in general requirement courses wind up lowering their standards to accommodate the deaf students who are far behind academically. Remember how earlier, I explained how some deaf children are stuck having to play catch-up for the rest of their academic careers, due to lack of communication during their developmental years? This, alongside the fact that it's impossible for every high school in the world to have an excellent deaf program, results in Gallaudet professors having a number of students in their class who can barely read a newspaper.

On one hand, I don't like seeing classroom standards lowered for deaf students, but on the other hand I understand the sticky dilemma some teachers have to adjust to. It's not easy to teach a class where half of the students are potential engineers or CEO's, and the other half can hardly read at the sixth grade level. Whereas hearing people can choose from many post-secondary institutions that best match their ability (be it a small junior college, large university or perhaps Yale or Harvard), there is only one university for the deaf. Gallaudet professors have to deal with all of us, for better and for worse.

No, I'm not implying that Gallaudet is the *only* option for deaf college students. Many deaf people can and do attend hearing universities, some of which have programs for the deaf. Nonetheless, a wide range of deaf people, with varying academic backgrounds, choose to attend Gallaudet.

For better, every deaf individual gets a chance to succeed at Gallaudet. For worse, a considerable number of good students are bored or insulted at having to take general requirement courses where the homework assignments look like junior high material. No, Gallaudet is not a junior high-level diploma mill; core courses related to your major, as well as most junior and senior year courses, are appropriately challenging. It is usually in a number of freshman/sophomore general requirement courses where teachers sometimes lower their standards. It gives the academically challenged students about two years to make the adjustment to bona fide college-level work. Some make it, some don't.

On an additional note, by the spring of 1995 there was an overhaul of some of Gallaudet's programs. Due to federally mandated budget cuts, it was necessary for the university to come up with what was called the Vision Implementation Plan. Designed for more cost-effective management of the university, the V.I.P. brought forth the elimination of some classes and programs that I felt had no place in a university. There has also been an innovative new program, known as Literacy 2000, which is being implemented to help students improve their English skills. Based on these moves and feedback from faculty and students, it is possible that standards at Gallaudet will be significantly raised, including admission standards. I know it could be argued that this might not be fair to some individuals who deserve a chance to catch up, but I agree that a university is a university and should have the standards thereof.

As time went by and I got my general requirement courses out of the way, I really began to enjoy getting deep into courses that were related to my psychology major. Outside of the classroom, I was catching up on missed social opportunities of past years by making a good number of friends. Of course, quality is better than quantity, and I found myself hanging out primarily with a very unique group of friends. This group consisted of Jeff Jones, Vijay Advani, Jason McKinnie, Derek "Heavy D" Gambrell and myself. You couldn't find a group anywhere with more differences than ours. Jeff and I are white, Jason and Derek are black, and Vijay hails from India. Jeff comes from a Catholic family, I come from a Jewish family, Vijay is Hindu, and Jason and Derek come from different Protestant denominations.

Nonetheless, living on the same floor in the Peet Hall dorm, we all became very close friends. We found that we all shared the same warped sense of humor, and bonded quickly. A Resident Assistant in Peet Hall pointed out that she thought it was amazing how people who were so different could get along so well. Jason, who was my roommate, just smiled and said,

"Hey... we're the family." I couldn't have said it any better. We really were a family. We didn't care about our differences; above all, we were Deaf first, everything else second. Our similarities in deafness overcame any differences in race or religion. In fact, we could share our experiences, both positive and negative, from our backgrounds. There was no right or wrong; there was no my-way-is-the-only-way righteousness that many supposedly religious people possess.

Often, usually on weekends, we would meet in room 206, where Vijay and Jeff were roommates. Unlike other dorm parties, however, ours were not always the wild, lampshade-on-the-head variety. Instead, we would stay up all night, watching movies and discussing philosophy until six in the morning.

The content of our discussions were so deep, that Jeff and I have often discussed taking notes and doing a whole book on them. It was amazing. We were all so different, united only in deafness... yet by the end of a good discussion, we would realize that we were all one and the same, no matter if white, black, Hindu, Catholic or Jew (if only everyone could learn how to appreciate this, what a better world this would be). On a surface level we could share similarities and learn from our differences, yet at the core we knew we were all brothers. There was plenty of laughter, plenty of frustration, plenty of support. It was very spiritual. There were countless times when one or all of us would come up with incredible philosophical insights. They came from within our hearts and out of the natural course of our conversation. We could come up with answers to why there was fear, hate, prejudice, discrimination and religious intolerance. We also came up with the solutions to those problems, all on our own. We felt that it was amazing how we could learn from each other and come up with such great concepts.

We weren't the first, however, nor will we be the last. Anytime a group of insightful people get together to relax and shoot the breeze, sooner or later someone comes up with something that makes everyone say "whoa, that's *deep.*" Far be it for me to imply that it was only our group which could do so. For all I know, my hearing friends might have had a group conversation going where they found the missing pieces to Einstein's Unified Field Theory. If they did, I must have missed it. With my Deaf friends, I missed nothing. There are certain dynamics in the group process where we can learn so much from each other, but this is possible only if we have full, unrestricted access and input. Sure, I had interpreters at Temple University, but I couldn't take them with me to late-night discussions in the dorm. My education there was limited only to whatever happened in the classroom. At Gallaudet, the learning experience ran 24 hours a day, seven days a week.

In the spring of 1990, most of my friends took off for a wild spring break in Florida, but I stayed behind. An old friend of mine back home told me he thought I had what it takes to play Division III baseball, even if it was more than five years since I last threw a pitch. I figured why not give it a shot, and signed up to try out for the Gallaudet baseball team. I came, I saw, I found I couldn't pitch like I used to... and made the team anyway as a shortstop. The experiences that would follow were amazing, and they also served as a microcosm for everything I needed to learn about Deaf culture.

As I routinely attended baseball practice, there was another awakening of sorts. In academics, when I attended my first class at Gallaudet, it was a big relief for me... because I remembered all of the stress I went through as the only deaf kid in high school. With baseball, however, I had *always* enjoyed the game, no matter who I played with. Yet I began to realize that the Gallaudet baseball team brought forth a new world that I never knew existed. Whereas on past ballclubs I would just show up and play, the Gallaudet team was an opportunity to be involved in everything, on and off the field.

Talent-wise, the best team I ever played for had to be the 1984 GFS team, which won its league championship; I really had a blast playing with them. Because I was deaf, though, I was never involved in any of the lockerroom banter or any of the pranks that went on. During road trips, I would be staring contentedly out of the bus window while the others were joking around. I never really felt bad about it. I knew I was deaf, and that was just the way it was. I was just happy to get a chance to play. I didn't really know what I was missing, anyway.

I didn't know what I was missing... that's what I now tell everyone who argues against my belief that deaf children should have the opportunity to interact with others like themselves. I have had many non-culturally deaf people tell me that they are doing great in the hearing world, getting by on oralism and never signing, and that they are happy and successful doing so. I, too, was once like that. I was proud of my status as only the deaf graduate of GFS, I was proud of my job at the supermarket, I was proud of my ability to interact with hearing people quite well… and *I just didn't know what I was missing.*

Being on the Gallaudet team more than woke me up to what I was missing; I experienced baseball as I never had before. Whereas on hearing teams I just did my part and went home, being on a Deaf team meant nine players united as one. The communication I was part of on the field was entirely new to me. The catcher would sign some instructions to the pitcher, who would then advise me, the shortstop, to be on my toes for what might happen next. I would keep the chain of communication going by turning around and being sure the outfielders knew what was going on. Often, I would be talking with the other infielders about what to do in various situations. The dialogue was continuous, a far cry from the days when I just stood there at whatever position I was supposed to cover.

Sometimes I would get a little weird, just to wake everyone up. Occasionally I'd give an outfielder a dirty joke in place of the usual strategic information I was supposed to relay, just to see if he was paying attention. I was able to be a leader or a clown, whatever the situation called for. I never really got to be like this on any hearing team I played for... I was enjoying every minute of it, on and off the field.

The stories about Gallaudet baseball could go on and on for an entire chapter or more. One of my favorites is the time our coach, Vance, got tired of us forgetting our signals while he gave them from the third base coaches' box. He usually ran off a complicated sequence of secret code signs, which included decoys, the indicator, the primary signal, and signs that meant "try it again" or "ignore previous signal." It got rather mind-boggling. On one occasion, a player who was on first base gave Vance a confused look as he received an array of signals. He was supposed to steal second base, but he repeatedly missed the sign. Vance sighed. Finally, he switched to signing in clear ASL, which the other team didn't understand anyway.

"Go ahead," he signed. "Steal second base whenever you want to." The player did, and the team erupted in laughter. There was also Vance's favorite "dummy" play, where he'd have a runner on first base purposely drift too far off the bag. The other team would try to pick him off, and then he'd suddenly take off for second base. During the ensuing rundown, a runner on third would zoom home and score.

We would laugh about all of these antics on road trips, and we would swap stories and jokes on the bus. We told a lot of Deaf jokes, we talked baseball, we talked about anything. I never knew that there was more to being on a baseball team than just doing what was supposed to be done between the foul lines. I never knew that a baseball team could be such a close knit family. *I didn't know what I was missing.*

If the baseball team gave me a taste of leadership skills, that was just the tip of the iceberg. A number of my classes were requiring group projects and presentations that required much teamwork and effort. Previously, I had been accustomed to just going along with whatever my hearing peers had decided to do. I was a puppet, the ultimate Yes Man with a hearing aid. At Gallaudet, this was no longer the case. My input was not only expected, it was highly valued. It took me a while to get used to this. I was so accustomed to being left out of group situations, that I would automatically zone out. My mind would just drift away whenever more than three people were discussing something. It was a natural habit of mine that was born out of necessity. Any time my hearing peers or family got together, I could only manage one on one conversations, sometimes two on one. When a group got together, that was it for me. I'd be bored out of my mind. However, going back to the brainwashing of my early years, it was always ingrained in my mind that deafness was bad and that I needed to be fixed. So I never complained when I was hopelessly lost in a group discussion. Instead of getting bored to tears, I just got into this habit where my mind would shut off from whatever was going on around me, and just entertain itself by flying off to some other world. I would be completely lost, but at least I wasn't bored stiff anymore. In a way, this functioned as a screen saver for my mind. Why waste energy having it turned on to the situation around me when there was nothing I could contribute? For that reason, I often zoned out. I was becoming a space cadet.

With my Deaf peers at Gallaudet, however, I had to unlearn this dissociative habit of mine. I would be very talkative in small groups or individual conversations, but in a large group I would by sheer habit just space out and have my mind fluttering all over the place. I would find myself snapping out of it and saying to myself, "Hey! Come back to earth! People are signing here, for godsakes..." I would realize that five or ten minutes of conversation had passed, and I had no recollection of it. I had to remind myself that I was in an environment where

I could understand everything. I was automatically shutting my mind down whenever there were a large number of people in the room. I was conditioned to react that way. As easily as Pavlov's dog started drooling, my mind could take off and fly to another galaxy.

Fortunately, there were plenty of opportunities for me to shake this maddening habit of mine. Hanging out with my best friends and playing baseball always kept my feet solidly grounded on this planet. Socially, I felt I was making good progress. Academically, I was always an excellent student individually, but still needed work on group leadership skills. Group projects and presentations enabled me to work on it somewhat, but I usually offered just enough to accomplish what was necessary, nothing more.

Finally, in 1991 I came across some experiences that helped me along even more. I applied for a job as Student Resident Assistant in Krug Hall, a freshman dorm. As part of the Student Life program, I was required to attend a number of professional growth workshops that demanded a high level of participation. It really introduced me to the dynamics involved in group and leadership situations. Not only that, I was expected to apply what I learned to my job as much as possible. In terms of solving individual or small group conflicts in the dorm, along with running special events, this was usually easy enough once I got the hang of it. It was really nice to be able to do this. In hearing schools, I never, absolutely *never* had the opportunity to do anything remotely like it. This was a good start.

The next step came shortly afterwards. I noticed that unlike previous years, I was facing challenges and dealing with them. No more slinking off to hide in the library because I was afraid to face choir class. Gallaudet offered many challenges, in and out of the classroom, and I faced them. I began to *crave* challenges.

One such challenge was offered by the Alpha Sigma Pi Fraternity, which I chose to join in the spring of 1992. Alpha Sigma Pi is a local fraternity that was founded in 1947; it was founded by and has always been run by Deaf students at Gallaudet. This was the perfect fit for me, as it represented everything I had gone through and come to believe in. After being pushed for so many years by hearing family and teachers, I felt it was an ideal situation for me to join an organization which was run by the Deaf, for the Deaf.

While pledging for Alpha Sigma Pi, I was required to work together with eleven other pledges. Sometimes it was hard but rewarding work, such as working in a soup kitchen for the homeless. Sometimes it was silly work, going through the crazy rituals that fraternities are known for. Some of the supposedly weird things we did actually had considerable significance, especially in areas regarding Deaf history. That was part of the fun. Alpha Sigma Pi's emphasis on Deaf culture contributed a lot to our personal growth. It was educational, it was fun, and it was zany.

Whatever we did, it was a great experience for me because I was learning everything there was to know about leadership and running an organization. I had balked at joining any organizations at GFS or Temple University, because I simply got left out. Besides, no one looked at me as an equal, as I was always "the deaf guy." I would have been the loner staring out the window while everyone else discussed something. With Alpha Sigma Pi, I was on the same wavelength as everyone else. I was expected to be as fully involved as anyone, and I was. I wound up becoming an officer, serving on the executive board and working as corresponding secretary.

Initially, I was in awe whenever the president asked me for advice from time to time. In the hearing world, I had been nothing but a bystander. I was not used to being involved in crucial decisions, some of which involved a considerable amount of money. I was not used to being asked to take risks and being responsible for them. These are skills you don't learn in the classroom, and they would come in handy in the real world after I left college.

There are some people who have responded negatively to my remarks about learning social and leadership skills at Gallaudet, arguing that college is not the kind of place where you spend thousands of dollars to socialize. While I was participating in an internet chat group, such an argument surfaced. I was pleased to see that it didn't take long for another Deaf person to jump in and point out that the lessons we learn outside the classroom are equally if not more important than the ones we learn inside. I can't emphasize this enough. We learn how to live life, the most important lesson of all.

Let's stop for a second and take a reality check. If you go back a few chapters in this book, you will recall how I graduated from one of the best high schools in Philadelphia. The quality of education at GFS was unbelievable. However, when I went to Temple University, I had no confidence in myself. I felt awkward around the thousands of hearing faces, and it took me a while to get settled down. I was shy and withdrawn, preferring to just go along with whatever it was that hearing people around me were doing. I had a strong foundation of academic skills, but never put it to good use. When I got the supermarket job in my neighborhood, I felt that was the end of the road for me... "not bad for a deaf guy." I was like a car without a starter. I was parked in neutral, going nowhere. I had the tools, but did not know how to live life.

Jump ahead to my senior year at Gallaudet, and look at the difference being with Deaf peers had made. I learned that I could influence other people, and that I could be a leader. I learned how to make decisions, instead of blindly following whatever others were doing. Most important of all, I learned to set my goals higher. No more "not bad for a deaf guy." I had seen many other Deaf people at Gallaudet go on to successful careers, and having these role models around meant a lot to me.

One such role model was not a fellow student, but a Deaf teacher, Ms. Childs. She was teaching a psychology course I was taking during my senior year, and she noticed I was coming down with a bad case of senioritis. I was getting a bit lazy with some assignments and had missed a few classes. Concerned, she called me into her office for a meeting. Let's just say that it was a friendly reprimand, a small kick in the rear. Basically, her message was "never be satisfied... shoot for more." If this advice had come from a hearing teacher, it might have gone over my head. I would have said "yeah, right, easy for you to say." But Ms. Childs was Deaf, and she had a degree from Harvard. She was telling me I could do much better. There was no way I could ignore her message. From that day on, I expected nothing but the best from myself. I was no longer going to sell myself short. Instead of perhaps going back to stocking shelves, I began to contemplate graduate school. A Bachelor's degree no longer appeared to be "not bad for a deaf guy"; I wanted a Master's degree. And then... who knows? My self-imposed glass ceiling was gone.

Granted, I began to expect more from myself in terms of academics and career possibilities. Socially, I had done the same; no longer the passive bystander, I had participated on the baseball team, joined a fraternity, and had the best group of friends one could ask for. Yet something was missing from the picture. I had yet to fall in love with a beautiful damsel, get married, have 2.5 kids and a dog, and live happily ever after. That was next on the agenda.

Before moving on to the sordid details of my love life at Gallaudet, let's conduct a brief review of my romantic endeavors in the hearing world. It will help you appreciate my (ahem) modest but meaningful relationships with the opposite sex at Gallaudet. In no particular order, here are some of the foul ups, bleeps and blunders of my love life in the hearing world:

- A three-year relationship with Karen, which shouldn't have lasted more than a year. It dragged on for eternity because hey, she signed. Couldn't ask for more than that.
- A rendezvous with a very attractive hearing girl during a party at St. Joseph's University. I could not understand one word she said. After a few beers, I forgot I was deaf. We got along swimmingly for the next two or so hours, until I threw up on her shoes. End of story.
- A woman from my neighborhood who knew sign language jumped into a serious relationship with me. One problem: she still had another boyfriend. We were all confused and didn't know what we really wanted. It was very awkward. Hey, she signed. I couldn't let go, let alone realize how stupid I was. Big mistake.
- At a Temple University party, I had the very rare thrill of two women competing for my attention.

One of them was the sweetest girl I had ever known. The other was a girl who signed fluently because she has a deaf brother. Unfortunately, this fluent signer also had a reputation for emotional instability. One guy specifically warned me not to get involved with her because "she'll bite you... she will really, really bite you." Of course, I go with the girl who signs. She tries to bite me, I flee the dorm at six in the morning... never to return again.

There were a couple others, but by now you've pretty much caught on to the common thread: my choices were very limited. Of those examples, a *lot* of time passed in between. In fact, two years of absolute drought passed between my first dysfunctional relationship and the second one. So I was often starved for love, and looking for it in all the wrong places. Whenever an opportunity came, I would grab it, no matter how ill-advised.

During my years at Gallaudet, however, I learned a new word: restraint. There were women everywhere, and they all signed. There would be no more settling for a woman just because I felt it was the best I could do. There would be no more clinging on to the rare ones who could sign, because at Gallaudet, *everyone* signed. And most of them didn't bite.

Lo and behold, I found plenty of opportunities for dating in my new environment. Wonder of wonders, I was actually being selective... if a certain woman didn't appeal to me, I didn't jump the gun. I had a few dates every now and then, but none of them turned into anything serious. I knew there would be others, and that I could wait for the right one to come along.

The right one came along in February 1991. Her name was Melanie McPhee, from British Columbia, Canada. Actually, she came along sometime in September 1990; I met her in the Peet Hall laundry room and was immediately smitten. But I had been on the receiving end of a false rumor that she already had a boyfriend, so I backed off. I had already seen what kind of disaster arises from dating someone who's already spoken for, so I wasn't going to make the same mistake twice. But there was no other mystery man in Melanie's life, and she was going crazy trying to drop me hints that she felt a mutual attraction. I think she had to rap me on the head and say something like "kiss me, you fool!" before I got the idea. Either way, we officially had our first date on February 1st, 1991. I haven't stopped dating her since, and she hasn't stopped rapping me on the head.

We began a unique relationship, and became quite an item on campus. We were known affectionately as "Melonhead and Drolz", and were practically inseparable. Many people remarked that we appeared to be made for each other, usually because Mel seemed to be the only woman capable of putting up with my weird sense of humor.

Finally, the insanity came to a climax on April 18th, 1992. My Alpha Sigma Pi brothers were hosting their annual Cobrafest party, which drew a crowd of 700 people. One reason for the huge turnout, other than the live bands and the delicious bratwurst, was the eagerly awaited raffle. We had sold a high number of raffle tickets, which offered students a chance to try their luck at winning a computer, VCR, television, and a number of other valuable items. This was nothing new; we do this every year. But this particular raffle was different... it was slightly rigged.

When the twentieth and supposedly final raffle number was drawn and the prize given to the lucky winner, everyone in the audience who didn't win began to shred their tickets and throw them in the air. As one of the officers who was on stage picking out winning tickets from the raffle wheel, I began to frantically sign,

"Hold it! Hold it! It's not over yet!" The entire crowd then stopped in its tracks.

"Due to the enormous success of our last party, Alpha Sigma Pi was able to add a twenty-first prize to this year's raffle." I held up a blank piece of paper and pretended to read from it.

"The winner of the additional mystery prize is... Melanie McPhee. Mel, come on up here..." Melanie climbed on stage, and the crowd looked on curiously. Many of the people in the audience were aware that Melanie was my girlfriend... either this was a fix, or something interesting was about to happen.

"Close your eyes, Mel," I began. "When I tap you on the shoulder, open them and see what the mystery prize is." She did as I told her. Immediately, two of my best friends, Tony Peeler and Jeff Jones, snuck up behind Melanie and unfurled a banner. The crowd immediately began roaring. As I tapped Melanie on the shoulder, she opened her eyes and was initially disoriented upon seeing 700 people cheering wildly. Turning around, there was the banner:

Melanie, Will You Marry Me?

Right on cue, I pulled out an engagement ring and slipped it on her finger. Dumbfounded, Melanie began crying as her Delta Phi Epsilon sisters jumped on stage and swarmed us. Some people in the audience began signing, "Well? Well?" Oops. Mel quickly turned around and gave the crowd an emphatic "YES!" and the party went on. Amidst the celebration, a teary Melanie grabbed me by the collar and began to sign discreetly.

"I'm gonna kill you."

As special as that moment was, it wasn't over yet. We returned to Melanie's dorm room at two o'clock in the morning, and she decided to call her mother back home in Fort St. John, British Columbia. What with the three-hour time difference, it would only be eleven p.m. over there, and this was certainly big news. Melanie gleefully shared the events of the past few hours with her mother over the phone. After she hung up, I was so caught up in the moment that I figured what the heck, I might as well call up *my* mother. So I began dialing. Meanwhile, I forgot that my mother does not live in a different time zone. Up in Philadelphia, it was two-thirty in the morning, same as in D.C. — oops. What ensued was the closest I have ever seen anyone actually mumbling on a teletypewriter (TTY):

"XCNMSSHERRY GA"

"HI MOM, BRAT HERE... GUESS WHAT? GA"

"HOLD... YOU WOKE ME UP LET ME USE TTY DOWNSTAIRS HD

LKMDOKAY... GA"

"SORRY TO WAKE YOU UP BUT I HAVE GOOD NEWS... I JUST GOT ENGAGED TO MELANIE A FEW HOURS AGO GA"

"ARE YOU DRUNK QQ GA"

"NO IM SERIOUS WE GOT ENGAGED AT THE ASP PARTY GA"

"...ARE YOU A FATHER QQ GA"

"NO NO WAKE UPPPP!!! IM GETTING MARRIED CUZ I WANT TO... DUHHHH GA"

"OH WOW! CONGRATULATIONS SORRY I AM SLEEPYHEADED WOW WHAT A SURPRISE WONDERFUL... "

Thus began a new chapter in our lives. It was anything but the ordinary. I wouldn't have had it any other way.

Chapter 8

After the wild events of the night I proposed to Melanie, I eagerly looked forward to getting married. I couldn't wait to make the jump from "I love you sweetheart" to "take out the trash," and from "you look so sexy" to "you got something yecchy in your eye." But it would have to wait just a little bit longer. Sure, I was about to graduate, but with a Bachelor's degree in psychology. In that field, a B.A. means you're now qualified to work the fries section at the local burger joint. Melanie and I agreed that perhaps it would be best if I went after a Master's degree before we tied the knot. This way I'd be more likely to land a good job, and thus would be more able to support us both when she eventually went after her Master's in Deaf Education.

In May of 1992, I walked across the stage in the Gallaudet Field House, shook President I. King Jordan's hand, and had my Bachelor's degree. It took me eight years of bumbling around, but I finally had a degree. I'm not sure if anyone was more excited than my grandmother, Rose, whose mantra over the past couple of years was *"I wanna see you graduate before I die."* My family shared the same joy, and got the unusual treat of seeing my two cousins, Trina and Daniel, also receiving their degrees that day.

For me, however, it was not really the same kind of celebration it was for my family. To them, it was the end of a long journey that took eight years. To me, it was just a stepping stone, more of a beginning. I was looking ahead to graduate school. I would be in Gallaudet's Department of Counseling, as a School Counseling and Guidance major. So there was no teary goodbye to Gallaudet, as I would be around for two more years. After taking eight years to get the Bachelor's degree, two more for a Master's degree wasn't asking for much. I was raring to go.

During the summer of 1992, my fiancée and I moved into a large apartment off-campus, rooming with my good buddy Jeff Jones and his fiancée, Cheryl Reinagel. We wound up running what looked like a kitty compound, as we took in a stray cat that had three kittens outside. Soon all four cats made themselves at home in our apartment, and the females, those harlots, kept going out for a good time and coming home pregnant. At one point, we would have eleven cats coming and going. It took a "free kittens" advertisement and lots of Lysol to restore sanity to our place. Melanie and I wound up keeping Shamu, a chubby black and white cat who resembles her namesake at Seaworld. Jeff and Cheryl kept Sierra, the calico that we originally found meowing at our doorstep.

In between frequent litterbox changings, I found myself nervously anticipating graduate school. Was I ready? Did I have what it takes? I was nervous, but nonetheless looking forward to the challenge. I wanted to know if I could play in the big leagues. The fact that I graduated from the undergraduate program Magna Cum Laude did not give me a sense that grad school would be a piece of cake. Far from it. Yes, I had learned a lot as an undergraduate, both in and out of the classroom. But there were no hearing students to compete with in the undergraduate program, and some of my earlier courses had me wondering if I actually had a watered-down Bachelor's degree. I needed to find out if Gallaudet had prepared me sufficiently for the tougher challenges that would await me in graduate school, and later, the hearing world.

It did. Graduate school took some initial struggling, but I adjusted as I went along and wound up doing quite well. My teachers could be very demanding in terms of coursework, but very supportive in terms of friendship and mentoring. It was an environment that was *very* conductive to personal growth.

My only problem in graduate school came in the first semester, when I had to learn how to upgrade my study habits. In the undergrad program, it was possible to do homework at the last minute and cram all night for exams. That gives you time to do all the crazy things undergrads are supposed to do, such as attending pep rallies and swallowing goldfish. Graduate school, however, is a full-time commitment, and I learned this the hard way. It would take a figurative smack in the face to wake me up.

With study and research skills which were still what one would expect to find at the undergraduate level, I compiled and handed in my first research paper, confident that it would rack in the "A" I had been so accustomed to getting. Oops, not so fast. It came back with an ugly "B-", and among the many red-ink comments was a scathing "this is not a graduate-level paper." Cripes! I seethed, and then I came to my senses. No more cruising along with the coursework, I realized. It was time to put my nose to the grindstone.

From that point on, I pushed myself harder. I learned that the best way to succeed in grad school was to go one step further than the teachers asked you to. This meant using more references, putting in more effort, adding an angle which no one had ever thought of before, and so on. I had barely eked out a "B" for a couple of my classes during the first semester, but from there on it was hard work followed by excellent grades. I had learned my lesson.

As it turned out, I was not the only person to benefit from my graduate education. My mother visited one day, and somehow wound up learning a few things herself.

She was in town for a workshop at Gallaudet, related to her work at PSD. During her free time, she was able to meet with me and do some shopping in the bookstore. At one point it was time for me to go to my Psychosocial Aspects of Deafness class, which was taught by Dr. Allen Sussman. I figured what the heck... why not invite mom along? She was always involved in anything related to Deaf culture back home, so I figured she would certainly get a kick out of this. This was the class where I learned about the "Diagnostic Crisis" mentioned earlier in this book. This kind of lesson usually resulted in my saying, "aha, so *that's* why so-and-so reacted to my deafness the way he did." It helped me learn more about myself and the people around me. With Dr. Sussman's permission, my mother sat in on one class. She would never be the same. Yes, she was in awe seeing a Deaf man with a Ph.D. teaching a graduate course, but what followed would really knock her off her chair.

The topic for that particular class was "Seven Attitude Dimensions As Measured By The Disability Factors Scale (Deafness)." Basically, we were reviewing certain attitudes that may lead to questionable behavior directed towards deaf people. There were seven listed on the handout, but on this day we covered in depth the ones known as "authoritarian virtuousness" and "imputed functional limitations." The official definitions, quoted as they appear in the handout, are:

Authoritarian Virtuousness: *This factor is distinguished by the over-favorability of the items. Despite the ostensible favorable tone of the content, it has a clearly unfavorable orientation. It pictures the able-bodied person as very warm and sympathetic toward deaf persons, advocates thoroughly favorable and preferential treatment of them, and ascribes special talents and* *personal traits to them, is full of sweeping and moralistic statements, and has a strong "do-gooder" flavor. It is, however, double-edged in that while endowing deaf persons with special qualities, it advocates tolerance for their shortcomings. Further, it imputes inferior status to deaf persons, suggesting benevolent superiority on the part of the nondisabled person.*

Imputed Functional Limitations: *Focuses on the ability of the deaf person to function adequately and effectively in the environment, in specific occupations, driving cars, and general capacity in response to surroundings.*

Shortly after we began to wrap up our discussion on imputed functional limitations, the insights began to hit my mother, the same insights that had already hit me. *Whoa... so that's why they treated me that way.* Immediately upon the end of the class, my mother thanked Dr. Sussman for what was a very fascinating lesson. She told him about her own experiences with imputed functional limitations, which Dr. Sussman would ask me to share with the next class. The story that stood out the most involves Episcopal Hospital in Philadelphia, where I had an operation to have tubes put in my ears.

My mother began explaining how one morning back in the early 1970's, she had taken me to Episcopal for the surgical procedure. It just so happened that my hearing grandfather, Martin, worked in a printing shop that was not that far from the hospital. He decided to drop in and offer his support before going off to work. He spoke to a few doctors briefly while my mother signed me in, and then he tried to calm me down by assuring me everything would be alright. I had been through this before, and was not too thrilled to be going through it again. Once I was wheeled into the operating room, there was nothing more my grandfather could do, so he left for work.

Meanwhile, my mother waited. And waited. And waited. Two hours passed, and no word on how the operation went. Three hours. It was getting unusually late. At the other hospitals where I had gone through the same operation, a doctor would immediately come out and tell my mother everything was fine as soon as the procedure was finished. On this occasion, however, a nurse kept peeking into the waiting room. She would make brief eye contact with my mother, then worriedly head back to the recovery room. It was getting on my mother's nerves. Finally, she managed to corral the nurse and ask her how I was doing. The nurse nervously insisted I was fine, and once again evaded any further contact.

Four hours after the operation had taken place (keep in mind the whole procedure takes only thirty minutes) and after several more tentative peeks into the waiting room by the nurse, my mother finally exploded.

"Where's my son?"

"He's in the recovery room, he's doing fine..."

"I want to see him," my mother angrily demanded. "NOW."

The nurse balked, but my mother would have none of it. Finally relenting, the nurse gave my mom the standard hospital gown and cap required for visiting the recovery room. Extremely agitated, my mother walked right into the room, and... found me surrounded by a bevy of beauties. I was wide awake, laughing and joking with three or four attractive nurses, teaching them funny signs like "the doctor is goofy." My mother was relieved, but also somewhat irked. What was this, romper room? My mother wanted to go home, and I should have been discharged hours ago.

"Why can't we go home now?" she demanded.

"Uh, I can't really tell you," the nurse squirmed.

"Look, you said he's fine... I've been waiting for four hours, so you tell me *now* why I can't take him home." My mother was positively steaming. The nurse stammered apologetically.

"I'm really sorry, but you can't take him..." she began. "You're deaf."

I must have been only eight or so years old at the time, so a good twenty years have passed since then. But I cannot recall ever seeing my mother angrier than she was at that moment.

"WHAT? WHAT KIND OF IDIOTS ARE YOU? THAT'S MY SON YOU'RE KEEPING FROM ME!" It suddenly dawned on her that the whole time the nurse kept peeking into the waiting room, she had been looking for my hearing grandfather, whom the hospital deemed the only person fit to take me home. Seething, my mother continued to argue with the medical staff. In the midst of all the confusion, one of the nurses eventually called our family doctor for advice. Upon learning of the atrocity that had been taking place, *he* exploded and gave the caller a tongue-lashing of his own. I was immediately discharged and went home with my mother.

Dr. Sussman marveled at the story, shaking his head at the ignorance of the medical staff. It was quite an example of imputed functional limitations. It's not that unusual to see people assuming that deaf people can't drive or hold good jobs, but here we had a case of medical professionals thinking that a deaf woman could not possibly be responsible for her own child.

My mother also remarked that years later, upon sharing that story, some of her friends would groan and tell her she should have sued the hospital. However, except for initially losing her cool, she just let it go. She felt that was just the way things were, and that there was nothing she could do about it. It was just the way hearing people could be sometimes.

But at this moment in time, she felt somewhat vindicated. A graduate class had just discussed in detail the types of inappropriate attitudes and behaviors that she had been subjected to, and there were even fancy psychological terms for them. She realized that she was not the only person to go through such experiences, and it was evident to her that there was no reason why she should have to put up with anything like it again. As Dr. Sussman would explain to the next class, "now she has a peg to hang her hat on."

Over dinner that evening, my mother and I would further discuss what we had learned together. Dr. Sussman was correct; she really did have a peg to hang her hat on, as she pointed out that she could relate to many of the examples discussed in class. The same insight kept popping up: *so that's why they treated me that way*. It was like someone had taken the blinders off of her and she was seeing social reality for what it was. We began to review some situations that had occurred in the past, and how they related to the attitude dimensions covered in class.

Quickly, flashbacks began to appear. The teacher in oral school who gushed *"oh that's so wonderful!"* when my mother barely managed to utter a sound. Never mind that the sound was incomprehensible and that the whole time this was going on, my mother and her class were far behind what would have been considered age-appropriate grade levels in academics. So that's why they treated me that way. The airline attendant who actually held my hand and walked me to my seat when I told her I was deaf... *so that's why they treated me that way.* The relative who, on a trip to Florida, smacked my mother's hand and admonished her for nearly wasting a quarter on a stick of gum. He had his own brand of gum in the car, and ordered her to put her preferred choice back on the counter. Big deal, you might say, but my mother was fifty-one years old when this happened... *so that's why they treated me that way.*

It was absolutely amazing how after just one class, everything sort of clicked and just made sense. The real kicker came from a separate handout, an article titled *Deafness: An Existential Interpretation* by Stanley Krippner and Harry Easton. One of the key excerpts:

If parents are not able to accept the fact that their child is deaf and continue to deny the implications of the deafness, the resulting effects on the child are to encourage his own denial and lack of authenticity. Such a child is thus unable to accept himself and his capacity to emerge or become a unique person is blocked. He lives an existential lie and becomes unable to relate to himself and to other deaf individuals and to the world in a genuine manner.

The above passage, in its simple beauty, explained *everything.* My frustrations and embarrassment, my unsuccessful struggle to fit in, trying too hard to please everyone, my inability to "emerge" despite an excellent academic background... *so that's why I treated myself that way.*

As the evening wore on, the topic shifted from the attitude dimensions to the question of why we put up with them in the first place, especially in the examples where we got it from our own family. For a considerable time, we just accepted it. If relatives in our family ordered us around like children, if they expected us to stay for the duration of boring social events where we had no inkling of what was going on, we usually complied.

By the end of my senior year at Gallaudet, however, I had stopped. I began to assert myself and stood up for my rights as a deaf person. Just socializing with my Deaf peers at Gallaudet had taught me that I deserved better than standing around with a phony smile. No, I would not alienate my hearing family and friends, I emphasized. Nonetheless, I would not subject myself to excruciatingly boring or uncomfortable situations, either.

If you go back a few chapters, you will recall that my social skills in the hearing world consisted of managing a few one-on-one conversations, and smiling like an idiot whenever I was lost in a group situation. If all else failed, I would occasionally get drunk and forget I was deaf. Not anymore. Whenever my hearing friends got together and I was invited, I got into the habit of always bringing along at least one other Deaf person. It could be Melanie, Vijay, Jeff, or my old pal from PSD, Michael Ralph. Sometimes it was all of them. Either way, I was not going to be the only Deaf guy standing there wondering what was going on. If by chance there were no other Deaf people able to accompany me, I would sometimes stop by and chat with my hearing friends for a brief time, and then leave when I had enough of trying to keep up with the conversation. Other times, when I just wasn't in the mood to do that, I would simply pass on the opportunity and not bother to go. The best thing about my new social philosophy was that I was no longer getting rip-roaring drunk. I would have one or two drinks, if any at all, and fully enjoy myself. No more Budweisers-for-boredom quick fixes. I was in control.

Normally, all of this shouldn't seem to be much of an issue. Surely, anyone could understand why a Deaf guy wouldn't feel like staying too long in a room full of hearing people who don't sign. But for all of those years before I went to Gallaudet, that's exactly what I did. I put up with it, and always gave the impression that I was happy where I was. With no Deaf peers around, I had felt that I needed to look and act hearing in order to be accepted. So I would grin and bear it in a number of social situations where I wasn't really comfortable. I did this so much that my hearing friends and family had become used to it. Now, all of a sudden, I was putting limits on my social appearances. Everyone must have thought, *what is it with that guy? He goes off to college for a few years, then comes back a total snob. He doesn't hang with us like he used to.* In fact, Dave, my best friend since little league baseball, somewhat half-jokingly remarked to me,

"Hey man, I thought you blew me off..." Oh, far from it. I would never blow anyone off, but things were going to be a little bit different from now on. It would take time to adjust, but we did, like good friends always do.

As I continued to discuss all of these deaf/hearing social dynamics with my mother, I actually began to confront her. It seemed odd to me that she was still putting up with awkward social situations that I no longer tolerated. It was odd because she has *always* had Deaf peers whom she could lean on for support. She grew up and went to school with other Deaf people. I, on the other hand, had been a hearing wannabe for many years, going to hearing schools (and trying to fit in) before eventually attending Gallaudet. So why was I doing what was fair and reasonable, while my mother was tolerating hand slappings and the dreaded "Dinner Table Syndrome" with her hearing family? At age fifty-one, for heaven's sake, you'd think she'd say *enough already.* Why not, indeed?

The only explanation my mother could come up with was that she came from a generation that was very oppressed, and got used to being oppressed. In her school years, teachers whacked anyone who dared to sign in class, as the oral method was strictly enforced. There were no prominent deaf role models to speak of, save for perhaps the relatively few "oral successes" whom most of the prelingually deaf could not emulate.

The lack of technology we have today (TTYs, relay services, assistive devices) further contributed to Deaf people being overwhelmingly dependent on the hearing to help them. Yet the hearing did not know how to provide the Deaf community with what they really needed, so the vicious cycle of oppression continued, regardless of how well-meaning some educators and medical professionals might have been.

My generation, however, was the Deaf President Now generation, one that was able to assert itself and stand on its own feet. So even though I joined my peers somewhat late, my mother surmised, it didn't take long for me to assimilate their social values and opinions. In fact, it didn't take long for the DPN generation to have an impact on my mother, either. Besides learning from my class and from talking about it with me, she had further conversations on similar issues with my good friends Vijay and Jeff. Impressed, she would go back home and tell her supervisor at work, Larry Brick (who is also Deaf), what she had learned. His reaction was somewhere along the lines of "Of course! Where have you been all these years?" He would assure her that it was alright to stand up for herself. Through all of this, my mother suddenly realized that perhaps she had been *too* tolerant of a lot of things. She knew she had to make some adjustments.

Lesson number one would be how to handle the "Dinner Table Syndrome," the phenomenon that occurs when there is a deaf person sitting at the dinner table with his or her hearing family. My father was lucky enough not to have to deal with this until he married my mother, since his own family was Deaf and anyone could participate in dinner table conversation. After getting married, however, he found himself joining my mother's family for dinner every now and then... and it was extremely frustrating for him not to be able to understand what was being said. He would eventually get tired of it, and it reached the point where he would rarely attend any of their gatherings. He just couldn't tolerate it. Later, when I was older, the issue came up again. All my father would say about it was: *someday, you will understand.*

Someday was now. I decided to bring up the Passover seder that my mother had dutifully attended every year of her life. I had something like a twenty-five year streak of my own going, but by my senior year it was snapped. During my grad school years, I didn't attend at all. I know, I know, that's awful. But I wasn't going to hop in the car, drive three hours up I-95, and then sit bored out of my mind for another three hours while my hearing family said and did things I could not understand. My family chose to look at it as "Mark can't make it because he has finals coming up" instead of "he won't come up because the environment here isn't very accommodating for a Deaf person." I told my mother that if we really emphasized the *real* reason we weren't happy with the seder, it would make it more likely that there would be positive changes in our favor. We just needed to face the problem instead of hiding from it.

"But we've gone for so many years," my mother argued. "They're used to us sitting through the whole thing and not complaining about it... and they're getting old, it's too late for them to understand." I disagreed.

"So," I began, "you'll have to just sit there for three hours bored out of your mind. You really enjoy that?" My mother shook her head no.

"So why put yourself through it? Why be the martyr? Work something out!" I proposed simple solutions. Number one, if she wanted to stay for the whole duration of the seder, simply hire an interpreter. Two, if an interpreter was out of the question, just ask what time the seder would start. If it was scheduled to start at six, simply show up at seven-thirty, which would be about the time dinner would be served. Enjoy the meal, say hello to the whole family, and just ask for permission to leave if the end-of-the-seder prayers were too much to sit through. If anyone protested, simply tell them the truth: "I am Deaf; it is hard for me to sit here and not understand anything."

Agreeing with me but somehow wondering if I was going overboard with the Deaf rebel routine, my mother once again consulted with her boss and mentor, Larry Brick.

"Of course!" he told her. "If my family had a large event and they expected me to attend, I would bring an interpreter." He handed my mother a copy of an old article he wrote for a parent newsletter. It was about helping deaf children cope with hearing family gatherings. Since he was Deaf himself and knew how it felt to be left out, he never put any unfair social demands on his own Deaf children. They worked out an agreement for family affairs: they would show up, say hi to the family, and politely join them for dinner. Once dinner was over and conversation began to drone on, the kids would discreetly excuse themselves. Then they would retreat to the TV or to the toys and magazines that they had brought along. Who could complain? It was common sense.

With all of this said and done, my mother did something she never had done in her entire life: prior to the next Passover seder, she spoke up for herself in front of her family. For the first time ever, at age fifty-two. She

154

actually asked my grandmother for permission to bring an interpreter to the seder. Grandmom, however, felt uncomfortable with this and declined; it would have felt weird bringing in a total stranger for such a special family event, she implied. My mother then countered with the argument that it was so hard for her to just sit there mindlessly while the whole family just talked and talked. Prayers were even worse; someone would try to help by sticking a book in my mother's face and pointing to the Hebrew that they were singing. This didn't help, because my mother could neither sing nor read Hebrew.

At the mention of this, my grandmother seemed to be hurt. It was too painful for her to admit that her daughter and grandson were totally deaf. It was easier to think that everything was alright. So when my grandmother looked up, she changed the subject and began talking about something way off the point. It was as if nothing happened. My mother and I looked at each other in sadness; the denial we just witnessed was very painful. Grandmom may have just switched subjects and gone about it as if nothing was ever said about our deafness, but we knew that deep down she was hurting. This was not going to be easy.

When Passover approached, I was back in D.C., so I called my mother on the phone and asked if she was going to go. She remarked that she had tried to talk about it one more time, and this time she actually made progress. Grandmom had finally, after all these years, admitted that she knew it was hard for us. She still wanted my mother show up for the whole duration, however. Her reasoning was that she needed help with setting up beforehand and washing dishes afterwards. I frowned. There are plenty of people who could do that. Why was it always my mom slaving in the kitchen while everyone else chatted over coffee? I argued with her that although she had made much progress in that they were now discussing the important issues at hand, the end result was the same. She was still going to show up for the whole shindig and would be bored to death. She admitted she really didn't want to, but... oh well.

On the day of the seder, however, my mother made history. She did not show up. She did what she felt was right... sort of. She called and said the dog was sick. When she informed me of this, I groaned.

"Oh right," I said. "You didn't go because the dog was sick. Even the dog knows that's not the reason." My mom laughed and pointed out that was true. It was just easier to make an excuse.

"Well, the dog *has* been ill lately," I pointed out. "So what are you going to do when she's gone? What next, you're not going to go because it's a bad hair day?" Mom laughed and we joked about other possible excuses. It was turning into a David Letterman Top Ten Reasons Not To Go To The Seder. We made a bit of a joke out of it, but it was no real laughing matter. Number one, we felt bad because we knew that we kind of blew off the family. There just had to be some kind of compromise. Number two, the dog thing just didn't cut it. Only the truth, as we all know, can set us free. And finally, number three, I realized I was pressing my mother too hard. She had made great strides; in fact, she would later be able to reach the reasonable type of compromise I had been pushing for. At future family events, she would inform the family that she would be staying for just a little while if she was going to be the only Deaf person present. If Melanie or I were there, she would stay longer. It would work out great, and I was proud of mom; after fifty-two years, she finally stood up for herself.

However, I also realized that I had been fighting my own battles with the family through my mother. Sooner or later, I would have to take a stand for myself as well. The time for that would come soon. Very soon. I knew that if I wound up settling down in Philadelphia after finishing school, the same issues would inevitably resurface with all over again with me. After all, after many years at Gallaudet, I had changed. I needed to express myself and everything I believed in, instead of passively going along with what others unrealistically expected from me. The Mark Drolsbaugh I really was and the Mark Drolsbaugh they wanted me to be were two completely different people.

In some ways, I was afraid that once I got out of school, seeing the real me might be too traumatic for my family. Whatever happened, I knew that I could no longer play the role of fake hearing person anymore.

Chapter 9

As expected, I rolled around the homestretch of my graduate program doing quite well. As enjoyable as it was, however, things began to get a bit crazy. While I was completing my studies, which included off-campus practicum and internship placements, I was also planning for the upcoming wedding and looking for job opportunities. Somewhere in the midst of all that, I was also doing an independent-study project that took me eight months to complete. It was a 175-page curriculum on health and wellness, which I put together under the supervision of Dr. Frank Zieziula. He was intrigued with the concept of holistic wellbeing and its relationship to counseling, and as the resident health nut of the university, I was thrilled to tackle this assignment. This project turned out to be a great release for me; I was able to throw myself into the topics I researched, such as exercise, nutrition, stress management, and meditation. Believe me, there is no better training a guy could go through prior to his wedding. This project, incidentally, was my last assignment of the year. Once I completed it, I had satisfied all of the requirements for a Master's degree.

Before we move from Gallaudet to the crazy challenges that awaited afterwards, there was one more experience in grad school that sticks out in my mind. In the spring of 1993, my practicum assignment was to work as a school counselor trainee at three mainstream schools in Rockville, Maryland. It was my first exposure to mainstreaming. Previously, my only experiences in education involved being the only deaf kid in a hearing school, and seeing what goes on in deaf residential schools. Besides PSD, I had also seen and observed classes at both Kendall School and Model Secondary School for the Deaf, which are situated on Gallaudet's Kendall Green campus.

Prior to settling down and working on my counseling skills with individual students in mainstreaming programs, I was permitted to observe a few classes. It was interesting to be in the mainstream environment, of which the Deaf community has always had mixed feelings about. Before getting a look for myself, the only things I had heard about mainstream programs were some less-than-favorable comments:

- They are socially restrictive, not offering social environments conductive to overall personal growth.
- Students have to deal with ignorance and discrimination from hearing staff and peers who don't know much, if anything, about Deaf culture.
- Due to the various limitations, students do not develop leadership skills, and lack thereof inevitably hurts them in the long run.
- Misinterpretation of PL 94-142 and subsequent legalities related to "Least Restrictive Environment" results in many excellent deaf students not being given a choice or a chance to attend good deaf schools. Consequently, the deaf schools lose valuable role models to mainstream programs, and the overall quality of deaf education declines. In essence, many deaf schools become dumping grounds for kids who couldn't make it in the mainstream.

Having been aware of all of the controversial opinions surrounding mainstream programs, it was with much curiosity that I observed a few classes at Barnsley Elementary, Wood Middle School and Rockville High

School. Some students attended regular classes with an interpreter, others attended special classes that were for deaf students only, and there were those who attended a combination of both depending on their needs.

The first class I got to observe was a group of twelve or thirteen year old deaf students at Wood Middle School. I was in for a surprise. They were going over their reading assignment, a story from *Aesop's Fables.* I smiled, as I recalled how my late grandfather had also read those stories with me when I was younger. Then the realization hit me.

Hey... these kids are reading material they're supposed to be reading.

I was dumbfounded. In my experiences with deaf residential schools, it was all too common to see many deaf students struggling to read material that was far below what would be considered age-appropriate. Yet these mainstreamed kids were reading the same material as their hearing peers. Inevitably, I began to question the quality of education in deaf residential schools. I recalled the time I wasn't permitted to transfer to a deaf high school as an eighth grader because I had already exceeded the academic level of all the *seniors,* for godsakes. How could this be permitted to happen?

My wide-eyed observations would continue at nearby Rockville High School, where I observed a group of deaf students reviewing and discussing in-depth material related to the Civil War. Unbelievable, I thought. Clearly, it was obvious that the mainstream programs in Rockville blew away any deaf school as far as academics were concerned.

Socially, the deaf kids did seem to be somewhat at a disadvantage compared to students at deaf residential schools, as their interaction was limited mostly amongst each other... a small group compared to the overall student population. They didn't seem to do that much with other hearing students, although there was a sizable amount of hearing kids in an ASL class at Rockville High. Regardless of the relatively limited social environment, this was still a heck of a lot better than being the *only* deaf kid in a school, like I was at GFS. Maybe there weren't as many situations where the kids could develop deeper social and leadership skills... maybe there was always the gnawing feeling that perhaps they didn't measure up to the hearing kids, who always made the football team or became class president.

I struggled with this and other pros and cons. Perhaps any social ramifications were negligible, as the kids could later catch up in an environment such as Gallaudet's or any local deaf club they could join as adults. Besides, if there were any social problems, that's what counselors were there for. We often addressed a number of social issues and had counseling groups related to adjusting to deafness in a hearing world. Most of the students, at least the ones I worked with, had a healthy and realistic attitude about their deafness.

By the end of my first week of working in the three mainstream schools, I vented out my frustrations about deaf education on my fiancée.

"Mel," I began. "All of my years at Gally, I've been so pro-Deaf culture. You know how I didn't really learn anything about myself until I came to Gally. You've seen me insisting that the best classes for deaf kids are the ones in deaf schools that use ASL all the time. So why are the mainstream kids kicking their butts? Those kids at Rockville are so far ahead of deaf kids in residential schools... their English ability is way better. What's wrong with residential schools?"

Melanie smiled, and shook her head. She has always been more level-headed than I ever could be. It's nothing new when I tend to get too emotional and miss the fine print with my arguments. Melanie, on the other hand, has this knack for staying grounded. She also happened to be majoring in education, so she had the resources to answer my questions and concerns. She sighed, reached for some educational handout she had stored away somewhere, and told me to read it very carefully.

I leafed through the handout and let out a long "ohhhhhh." It contained the findings of an extensive study which revealed that most prelingually deaf children tend to have the same reading and writing levels, regardless of whether they were in a residential or mainstream school. Oops. In the midst of all of the academic achievement going on in the mainstream schools, I had overlooked that factor. I realized that most of the students who had blown me away with their excellent reading and writing skills were in exactly the same boat I was in years earlier. Many of them had a significant amount of residual hearing and speech ability, which helped them pick up language in their most crucial, formative years. Thus they were not too far behind their hearing peers, if behind at all.

"But what about..." I mentioned a prelingually deaf student at Rockville who had also exhibited superior academic skill.

"Are her parents Deaf?" Melanie asked. I smiled. Indeed, they were. Melanie then asked me to name a few prelingually deaf students at Gallaudet who went to residential schools and were from Deaf families. I began to name a few. Among them was Kelby Brick, Larry's son... who graduated from MSSD, then Gallaudet, and went on to law school. In fact, all of the people I came up with were either in grad school or already holding good jobs. Ohhhhh. It took a while, but Mel finally got her point through to me. Upon taking a closer look, I realized that there were some prelingually deaf kids in the mainstream program who did not come from families that used sign language. They *were* significantly behind everyone else.

My conclusion? I cannot fully answer which is better... mainstreaming or residential schools. I can, however, identify the bottom line: the deaf child's access to language during the crucial years between age 0 to 5. This responsibility, ultimately, falls upon the parents, not the type of school program. If a child is hard-of-hearing with significant hearing and speech levels, he or she may establish enough of a language base (and consequent cognitive development) to be close or equal to his or her hearing peers. If the child is prelingually deaf, it is very crucial that the he or she is consistently exposed to ASL, in essence picking up the most accessible language. The formula is simple: no language equals no learning. If there is neither language nor learning in the first five years of life, a child will spend the rest of his or her academic career trying to catch up.

This explains why there are many prelingually deaf adults today who can only read at the third or fourth grade level. I cannot emphasize this enough... if a child is prelingually deaf, exposure to ASL and the opportunity to use it is extremely important. Only the parents can see to it that this is accomplished. A more sobering fact: at a recent workshop, it was revealed that for virtually all children, ninety-two percent of learning occurs at home. There is only so much a school can do to bring a child up to par if it isn't happening at home.

All things considered, it is still hard for me to pick sides between the varying educational programs. Overall, I would say that residential schools potentially have much more to offer. Keep in mind, however, that each kid is a unique individual. Some are more comfortable in one environment than in the other. There are many other factors that come into play, such as quality of curriculum and signing ability of the teachers, so there is no black-and-white answer. Rockville High School, for example, had two Deaf teachers who were very fluent in ASL, and these two teachers were among the best that I had seen anywhere. With this in mind, along with all of the pros and cons of mainstreaming versus residential schools, I would have to say it comes down to a combination of the child's preference, quality of education, and potential for social-emotional growth.

Chapter 10

During the summer of 1994, Melanie and I flew up to her hometown of Fort St. John, British Columbia, for our wedding. Melanie's mother, Margaret, had handled most of the dirty work by the time we arrived. She did a fantastic job of seeing to it that everything was taken care of, and she made sure that all visitors, including my family, were comfortable and enjoying themselves.

Melanie's sister, Shawna, also did her share of work, and then some. In addition to assisting with all of the planning and coordinating, she graciously agreed to do a twelve-hour round trip drive to Edmonton, where she would pick up my friends Jeff Jones and Tony Peeler (who were groomsmen for the wedding) and bring them back to Fort St. John.

She also had to deal with getting busted by the Canadian police, the famous RCMP, for taking my rental car on the trip. The car was registered in my name only, and as Murphy's Law would have it, the police were conducting a random checkstop on the highway. Shawna was fuming, and it took a while to get out of that mess, but that's a whole 'nother story. Hey Shawna, we love ya.

Meanwhile, Melanie's father, Bob, had also added some unique touches of his own for the wedding. A collector of antique automobiles, he prepped up two of them for the wedding procession: a 1964 Studebaker convertible and a 1965 Chevy Supersport. We were going to go in style, that was for sure.

It was a great change of pace to be in Fort St. John after all of the craziness back in the States. Fort St. John happens to be on mile 42 of the Alaska Highway, so you can hardly get any further away than that. Whether it was sitting out back enjoying the clear night sky and the

Northern Lights, or relaxing indoors with Melanie's family, I was getting a much-needed break from the hassles back home. I'm telling you, it's no surprise that we never see Canada in the news that much back in the States. Perhaps we see so much coverage about war, disaster and political struggles in other countries, but rarely do we hear about Canada, our quiet and friendly neighbor. They're too busy being real, genuine people up there. In Fort St. John, people smile, say hello, and leave their car running while they go into a convenience store to buy a newspaper. Try that in New York, eh?

On July 16th, Melanie and I had a beautiful wedding in St. Luke's United Church. It was not, however, without its fair share of drama. Prior to the big day, a number of people in my family had expressed displeasure at the fact that the wedding was going to be in a church. On one hand, I didn't want to hurt their feelings, yet on the other hand I didn't want to disrespect Melanie's family and the church they had gone to all their lives. I scratched my head in bewilderment. We could've had a moonie wedding at the airport and I would have been happy. I was getting tired of these religious issues. The way things were going with the church arrangement, I felt a disaster was imminent. Religion was like water, I realized. Capable of nourishing, replenishing, and giving life... and also capable of causing mass destruction. Oy vey. What to do?

Out of nowhere, I heard a voice from the past. *There is no number one... except God.* It was Grandpop. He had always warned about how sometimes, in our desire to be the best, to be absolutely right, we alienate those around us. Yes, we should always be the best we can be, but not at the expense of others. It does no good to society when we're too caught up with stuff like my team is better than your team, my country is better than your country, my religion is better than your religion, my dad can whup your dad's butt, and so on.

I smiled, and I knew that Grandpop would always be with me. He was the religious leader of the family, and his word would never be questioned. I scribbled "there is no number one except God" on a piece of paper and handed it to my mother. In the event that anyone took offense to the way the wedding was conducted, she would give them the note and it would save the day. Call me paranoid, but the earlier rumbling and grumbling had me on edge. I wanted to be prepared for just about anything.

Needless to say, the wedding turned out to be very beautiful, and the aforementioned message was never needed. I'm going to have to disappoint the tabloid world by reporting that everything went just fine, without a hitch. In this age of trash TV, it would be tempting to write that all chaos broke loose. Like, say, my family interrupted the wedding... a woman from my past showed up with a kid looking just like me... my long-lost twin brother appeared out of nowhere to insist that it was he who really loved Melanie... nahhhhh.

To the delight of everyone, the wedding was absolutely beautiful. The only suspense came from Melanie's seven year old nephew, Donovan, who wasn't too comfortable with the idea of being ringbearer. His mother, however, bribed him with a lego set, and he kept his end of the deal. He performed his duties as ringbearer perfectly, and was very patient during the long photo session afterwards. I made a mental note that next time someone in my family raised any objections, I would buy them a lego set.

Seriously, the whole thing went perfectly, bordering on surreal. Melanie looked positively radiant, and I was in a daze. As Melanie and I exchanged our vows, both families beamed with pride and joy. I kicked myself for worrying that my family would object enough to interrupt anything. Sure, we had our differences of opinion, but above all, we loved each other immensely. I noticed my grandmother, Rose, grinning from ear to ear. She was genuinely happy for me, and had conducted herself with great dignity. She had, in fact, shown beyond a doubt that her love was unconditional. In the past, I had for whatever reason felt that I always needed to win her approval, to be hearing, to be this, to be that. Today, she had effectively shown that she loved me no matter what. I had not only gained a wonderful wife, but also a more genuine love and respect for my family.

After the wedding and a great vacation in Vancouver, it was time to come back to Earth. Melanie and I returned to Maryland, where a number of changes awaited us. Our roommates, Jeff and Cheryl, got married three weeks later in Buffalo, New York. Shortly afterwards, they moved out to live in a place that was closer to Gallaudet. Melanie and I were set to do the same thing, but there was one problem: I couldn't find a job anywhere.

Up in Canada, I looked around Vancouver for any available school counseling positions, but there were none. Back east in Maryland, I had certainly made a name for myself, but so did thousands of other Deaf people. Because of the close proximity to Gallaudet, there is no shortage of Deaf people with advanced degrees in Maryland. The competition for jobs in Maryland's Deaf community is therefore extremely tough. In Pennsylvania, there were two openings, but they were for a coordinator and a case manager in a mental health center. Not exactly what I had studied for, but close enough for consideration.

Before I threw in the towel, there was an ironic twist of fate. A very good friend of mine, Michael Ralph, left his job as school psychologist at PSD to accept a similar position at the Lexington School for the Deaf. That meant that there was an opening in the Evaluation, Enrollment and Counseling Center at PSD, and soon they contacted me. Although I'm a school counselor, not a school psychologist, PSD still decided to hire me. They had one other school psychologist and also another school counselor, but that counselor would be going on maternity leave the following year. Throughout all of this shuffling, they decided to hire another school counselor, which turned out to be me. I would provide individual and group counseling services, crisis intervention, case management, and occasionally assist in procedures related to enrolling new students. Once again, PSD was going to play a major part in my life.

Although there were a myriad of topics covered in both individual and group counseling, one thing that struck me quite hard was the prevalence of family issues, particularly those related to communication barriers. I realized right away that my problems paled in comparison, because at least I had Deaf parents and a Deaf wife who knew where I was coming from. Most deaf children, however, are the only such people in their families. This is especially evident around Christmas time, when PSD has a twelve-day break. It was prior to this break one year when I learned that some students have a considerably frustrating home life. While numerous staff and students had broad smiles on their faces, eagerly anticipating their vacation, there was a young girl who caught my attention. As fourteen year old Lori passed me in the hallway, I wished her a happy holiday and told her to enjoy the break.

"Oh, BORING!" She shot back. "I don't wanna stay home for twelve days!"

"Really?" I asked. "Aren't you glad to get a break from all the hard work you've been doing?"

"Yeah, but at home it's BORING!"

"Why do you say that?"

"Because no one in my family can sign... stupid family, boring!"

That explained it... I should have known. In the midst of all the holiday cheer, in my own excitement to escape the blahs of the rat race, I had completely forgotten that for some people, the holidays can be quite frustrating. Lori was going to be twiddling her thumbs for twelve days.

I could not imagine how tiresome it must have been for her. Lucky me, I go home with my Deaf wife and we can visit our Deaf friends anytime. And again, my parents are Deaf, as is most of my father's family. Although communication can be a challenge with my mother's hearing family, it's not that bad; there are usually more than two Deaf people present who can keep each other company when that side of family has an event. Besides, should it get too boring, Melanie and I are grown adults who can get up and leave whenever we want to. Lori, on the other hand, has none of the above, no such freedom. Asked to explain how that felt, she put her index finger between her lips and twiddled it up and down. *B-b-b-b-b-b-b-b.* That pretty much says it all.

After the break was over, Lori was thrilled to be back in school, as were many of her classmates. I decided to ask them how their vacation went. Most of them said it was alright, as they shared stories of eating delicious food and getting new toys for Christmas.

Lori mention that she, too, enjoyed the food and gifts, but she also felt left out when she had to sit silently at the table as her hearing family chatted non-stop. I smiled and remarked that this was a common phenomenon in the deaf community known as the Dinner Table Syndrome. I asked the class how many of them ever had to sit at a family

172

gathering and just smile politely, oblivious to all the conversation around them. Every single hand in the classroom went up. Lori's eyes widened in surprise as she realized that her problem was not unusual for most deaf people.

"I sit there like a statue," said one student.

"I ask my mom what people say, but she says 'nevermind' or 'it's not important'," said another.

"My mom signs, but no one else in the family does."

"I can talk to my deaf brother, but that's it."

"I want to watch TV but mom yells at me if I leave the table."

"I can lip-read, but only with one person at a time."

And so on, and so on. Every student had a story about how he or she tolerated the Dinner Table Syndrome. Lori was not alone. Now that we all identified the problem, it was time to look for a solution. So what could we do? The class came up with the following possibilities:

- Encourage your family to learn sign language.
- Negotiate; tell your parents it's not fair to be expected to sit for an extended period of time with hearing people who don't sign. Get permission to excuse yourself so that you can go play a game, read a book, or watch TV.
- Invite a deaf friend or relative over, so you have someone to talk to.
- For really big, special events, ask for an interpreter.
- During a long vacation, arrange to visit deaf friends and classmates as much as possible.

These are all excellent ideas that I definitely support. As usual, the students had shown their insight and creativity in such a way that it was I who learned from them instead of the other way around. They were absolutely right; with a little awareness and sensitivity, we can form a reasonable bridge between the deaf and hearing worlds. I knew I was going to enjoy working with them.

Regardless of the many enjoyable and enlightening moments, however, I wound up realizing that life as a counselor is not always easy. This is a job where one hundred percent success is virtually impossible, and that's something that drives me nuts. If you're a computer technician, you can fix computers and program them to do whatever you want. If you're a mechanic, getting a car to run properly may only be a spark plug away. If only it were that simple with people!

The truth is, with people there is no quick fix; instead there is a process, and a lengthy one at that. Human beings, after all, are very complex. We do not get cured, fixed, or repaired as quickly and efficiently as machines. We may experience success, and then just as quickly backslide and have lapses in judgment. On New Year's Day we promise we'll exercise more and eat less junk food, then two days later we're couch potatoes again. We improve, relapse, improve, and relapse again. Hey, we're *human*.

If you're a counselor and you expect to save the world, fix everyone's problems, and watch everybody live happily ever after, be prepared to bang your head on the wall. In counseling, you cannot become too attached to the results. You need to do the best you can, and then move on. Expect to take two steps forward, one step back, two steps forward, one step back… and eventually, over the long run, seeing that some goals have been reached.

Admittedly, this is hard for me because I like to see results, and I like to see them *now*. In all of my other jobs, success was directly proportional to how much effort was put in. Not so in counseling. There are times when constant effort brings forth minimal results, and conversely, times when one quick, impromptu session elicits incredibly positive results.

Another challenge is that regular counselors like myself sometimes have to take on cases that go well beyond what we were trained for. If a child is deaf and also has other mental or physical issues, that child is usually considered deaf first, everything else second. When the choice comes to placing that child in an environment with an appropriately trained clinical staff that does not sign, or in a communicatively accessible deaf school, the deaf school often gets the nod. And Joe Average counselors like myself often have to learn as we go along, sink or swim. So besides teaching social skills, problem-solving skills, study skills, sex ed, drug awareness and generally helping kids prepare for high school, we also get to work with cases involving maladjusted behavior, physical and sexual abuse, and other issues of a more clinical nature.

Incidentally, for all of you school counselors out there, don't try this at home. My former professors at Gallaudet made it quite clear that clinical cases are supposed to be referred to clinical professionals, and I agree with them. Unfortunately, the demand for services goes far beyond the supply of qualified therapists who sign.

However, if there's a place to take on such challenges and grow from the experience, it's PSD. Pardon my lack of modesty, but I believe we have the best support staff and resources anywhere. The key, in my opinion, is excellent teamwork and supervision.

In the Evaluation, Enrollment and Counseling Center, I have had the good fortune of working closely with Lisa Santomen, the Coordinator of Counseling Services. My life as a counselor is so much better because Lisa is a true pioneer. Before she became Coordinator of

Counseling Services, she worked full-time as a counselor herself, and she noticed there were more and more cases of a clinical nature popping up at PSD. She knew that more resources were needed, much more than what was available at the time.

Coincidentally, Dr. Annie Steinberg, a pediatrician and certified child psychiatrist, had already contacted PSD. Dr. Steinberg, unbeknownst to Lisa, was concerned about the exact same issues. Already fluent in ASL and having worked with several people in the Deaf community, Dr. Steinberg could see the need for additional services. She met with Headmaster Joe Fischgrund and proposed setting up what is now known as The Partnership Program, a collaboration between PSD counselors and mental health professionals from the nearby Philadelphia Child Guidance Center.

One of these professionals is Sam Scott, a dynamic family therapist who has many years of experience working with deaf children and their families. Sam was already giving workshops related to family therapy at PSD around the time Dr. Steinberg suggested setting up The Partnership Program.

Finally, the pieces began to come into place. Lisa, who was continuing to work with increasingly complicated cases, found her caseload including a significantly higher number of students with a history of sexual abuse. She contacted Sam, who in turn referred her to Cass Lavin-Spause, a therapist who specializes in treating victims and perpetrators of sexual abuse. Lisa and Cass teamed up and worked together for three years, providing much-needed clinical services to deaf children. The benefits of such a professional collaboration was obvious, and The Partnership Program was off and running.

And today, whenever a counselor at PSD winds up dealing with clinical issues, top-quality support is easily accessible. Dr. Steinberg visits the school for monthly consultations with staff and is always available by phone; she also accepts clinical referrals for cases that are way beyond what we were trained for. Sam works at the school regularly two or three days a week, and is also on call whenever an emergency situation arises. Both of them, thanks to their expertise and signing skills, have an excellent relationship with PSD staff, students and their families.

The best thing about this arrangement is the fact that PSD counselors, slowly but surely, become competent in areas that textbooks alone simply cannot prepare anyone for. In my case, on several occasions I have worked with Sam in family counseling sessions, sessions I never would have been able to run by myself. By allowing me to participate, Sam gives me the opportunity to learn in the best way possible... through experience.

Similarly, Lisa is always looking for ways to give counselors the opportunity to grow. She has an uncanny knack for assigning cases based on what she knows you are ready for. She provides regular feedback that proves to be very helpful, but the best thing is she allows you the freedom to improvise. Many traditional counseling activities, I've found, don't always fly with certain groups. So if I have a gut feeling to try something new, something different, something crazy, Lisa lets me do it. If it works, we will discuss why it was successful. If it bombs, we will discuss what happened, why it bombed, and what could be modified to make it work next time. On several occasions, a failed experiment became a rousing success after a "back to the drawing board" meeting with Lisa. This environment is a professional's dream: both success and failure equally contribute to the learning experience.

Put all of these great people and experiences together, and you have a safe environment where you are encouraged to develop your own style based on your individual strengths. My strength is improvisation and a goofy sense of humor, and I get to use both as often as I can. Lisa and Sam have influenced me greatly in the way I have developed as a counselor, and I would like to share some experiences related to this.

Sam, at first glance, appears to be somewhat unorthodox at times. He is not afraid to rock the boat, if that's what it will take to solve a problem (out of chaos comes order, as the old saying goes). And he does it in such a unique way that it's alright with everyone involved. He stresses that before he "pushes" someone, he will invest in the relationship first, in essence "putting money in the bank." Sam has this incredible ability to establish rapport, connect with a client, and then say or do something no one else could get away with.

Generally, if you are too blunt or plainly point out what people are doing wrong, they naturally get defensive. Yet Sam has a way of working around this, and people wind up hanging on to every word he says. I consider myself very lucky to be able to work with him and have stored plenty of "Sam-isms" in my mind: *"It's all about relationships," "You need money in the bank," "They've got your attention, now go get theirs," "Everything is recoverable,"* and *"Everybody wants one thing: to be understood."*

No doubt, if you've read this far, you're wondering what in blue blazes I'm talking about. The only way to show you is to give some actual examples of how this philosophy is put into practice.

Example #1: In a family session, a mother and father are overwhelmed by their increasingly rebellious teenage son's behavior. Sam connects with the parents by immediately demonstrating he understands how they're at their wits' end (*everybody wants one thing: to be understood*). He mimics the boy's behavior and acknowledges how it must be driving the parents up the wall (eliciting laughter from the parents, establishing rapport – *money in the bank*). He also demonstrates understanding of the boy's perspective, a young teenager seeking independence (*money in another bank*). He asks both parents and the boy what they want, valuing their opinions (*it's all about relationships*). He compliments the good ideas they have and encourages them to try them (*more money in the bank*).

And then, at this juncture, he corrects an error in the parents' approach. Normally, this might elicit a defensive reaction, but Sam has already found a way to correct that error with a solution the parents themselves came up with. He has plenty of money in the bank, so to speak, and is able to take a risk. It works. A win-win scenario is developed, as the boy will get what he wants so long as he heeds his parents' wishes and stays within the boundaries of their rules. Sam closes the session with his usual sense of humor: "Alright, you can either hug your parents, or you can hug me." The boy hugs his parents.

Example #2: Anytime a child acts out, Sam is quick to remark "okay, now he has your attention. Before you can work with him, you have to turn it around and get *his* attention." For me, this is usually the fun part of the job. On one occasion, a nine-year old boy threw a tantrum and bolted out of class. I happened to be walking down the hall nearby when the boy ran straight into my path. Startled, he skidded to a halt. Standing only two feet away from me, he dropped into a Kung Fu stance. This kid definitely had my attention. I knew that a rational response

would not work. It was irrational behavior, after all, so...
it earned an irrational response.

"No, no, no, no," I said, slapping my head in mock
disgust. "You got it all *wrong*. You have to hold your left
arm like *this*, otherwise you expose your side to a
counterattack." I corrected his Kung Fu posture, even
though I don't know the slightest thing about Kung Fu.

"Drop down a little lower," I continued. "There,
that's better."

And now, I had *his* attention. I bowed peacefully,
and the boy bowed back in kind. He calmly turned around
and walked with me back to his class, ready to meet with
his teacher and accept the consequences for his behavior.

Example #3: Two students in one class were at each
other's throats. Normally, you can't force anybody to be
friends, and if two people just don't like each other, fine.
But these kids were in a small classroom that consisted
of only four students, meaning half the class was in
constant chaos. If they could have just ignored each other,
it might have been okay, but they were hurling insults
and being very disruptive. Life was hell for the other
students, not to mention the teacher. The issue was brought
to Sam's attention, and he recruited me for help with a
wacky plan. He noted how the two students were both
hard of hearing, Hispanic, and extremely bright. Lecturing
them on the importance of cooperating with each other
was not going to work (it had been tried before), so it was
time for Plan B.

Sam and I abruptly pulled the two students out of
class (with the teacher's prior consent, of course). We
took them down the hall to Sam's office. We sat them
down across from us, and... ignored them. Instead of
talking to them, Sam and I took on the roles of the two
boys... and we began arguing with each other. We called

each other names, made fun of each other's bad habits, and so on. The two boys watched the whole show in amazement (hey, we had their attention). Then just as abruptly, Sam and I stopped and switched gears.

"Hey, you're hard of hearing... me too."

"Hey, you're Hispanic... me too."

"Hey, you're good at math."

"Hey, you're good at writing."

"Know what? Together we can show the whole school that we're number one."

"Yeah, Hispanic and hard of hearing, we rule!"

Sam and I shook hands, and then we got up and left. Throughout the whole show, we never talked to the two boys. We left them sitting there in total confusion. The lecture they were expecting never happened. They looked at each other as if to say, *what the hell was all that about?* They stayed in Sam's office for two minutes, trying to figure out what was going on... *together.* They got up and looked for us... *together.* They found us in my office... *together.* They both demanded to know what was going on... *together.* Sam and I simply shrugged. We categorically denied any knowledge of what had just taken place. And the two boys walked back to class together, discussing how Sam and I were either stupid or crazy, or both... *together.* Mission accomplished.

Note: There is indeed a method to the madness. For a more detailed look, grab a copy of *My Voice Will Go With You: The Teaching Tales of Milton H. Erickson* (edited by Sidney Rosen). Sam Scott had the honor of meeting and training with the late Dr. Erickson, and has incorporated some of his techniques. Wacky, but effective.

Example #4: This one has Lisa's fingerprints all over it. She is the master of reframing, the art of getting kids to take a different, healthier look at things. Without trivializing the kids' issues, Lisa has this way of changing their thought process so that they can see they have accomplished more than they have given themselves credit for. After watching her skillfully defuse countless situations, I had an opportunity to try it for myself.

Larry, age eleven, is notorious for pushing everyone's buttons. If there is a way to tick you off, he will find it. On many occasions, he goes too far, gets caught, and winds up in the Time Away Room. One day, I passed the Time Away Room on my way to a group counseling session, and noticed Larry was there again. I wondered what he had done this time. Two minutes later, I had my answer.

As I passed a classroom down the hall, a student jumped out of his seat and called for me. Derrick, age thirteen, was steaming mad. As he corralled me in the doorway, he vented profusely about Larry's antics. Larry laughed at his haircut. Larry made fun of his clothes. Larry gave him the finger. Larry made one too many "your momma" jokes. Larry...

"Wow," I interrupted. "I've never seen you so mad... Larry must have really pissed you off!"

"He did!" Said Derrick. "Larry got me so mad I want to kick his ass!"

"It certainly must be frustrating when he does that," I acknowledged. "But hold on a second. Where is Larry right now?"

"The Time Away Room."

"I see. And where are you?"

"I'm in my classroom and..." Derrick suddenly realized where this was going. He broke into a huge grin.

"Alright," I said. "Who's The Man?"

"I am!"

"Who stayed in control?"

"I did!"

After being congratulated for maintaining his composure throughout Larry's taunting, Derrick returned to his seat, absolutely beaming. The only thing that had really changed was his perception of the situation. Good enough for me.

After settling down at PSD with various counseling and school-related responsibilities, I also signed a contract to work for PSD's Center for Community and Professional Services, located right across the street. For CCPS, I work in the AIDS Education Program, which involves traveling to other schools and community centers to educate the deaf community about the dangers of HIV. Although I spend most of my time in my school counselor role at PSD, the job as AIDS educator has really opened my eyes to a serious social phenomenon we all need to be aware of.

Throughout this book I may have expressed regret over missing out on a number of things while growing up in the hearing world, but at least they were things I could get over or compensate for later. AIDS awareness, however, is one thing no one can afford to miss out on. There is no second chance. It scares me to see so many deaf kids with little or no knowledge of this dreaded disease. One child said that it was impossible to get HIV the very first time you have sex; another thought that HIV was transmitted exclusively through anal sex. These misconceptions, and many others, could be very deadly. I had never been aware of such a lack of information going around, and joining the AIDS Education Program proved to be one of the most rewarding and meaningful experiences I've ever had.

Around the time I became employed at PSD, my wife and I got a modem for our computer. Thus began another unique experience, surfing the 'net. Through our America Online account, we began to explore the vast expanse of the internet world. To our delight, there were newsgroups and mailing lists such as deaf-1 and Edudeaf, among others. We found deaf and hearing people from all walks of life sharing their experiences and opinions related to deafness. Remember that Deaf Chat Syndrome I mentioned earlier? With the advent of technology, it has now gone online.

When I jumped in and began participating in deaf-1 (which I still do under my America Online screen-name of "Deffman"), I initially stated my opinion that ASL and interaction with deaf peers is the solution for all problems facing deaf children today. Naively, I expected such a comment to be warmly welcomed by everyone. It wasn't. Granted, there were many positive responses, but I also got flamed to bits... by other deaf people. A number of them were oralists who had no interest at all in ASL and the capital-D Deaf community as we know it. Some of them were deaf people who signed, but nonetheless considered themselves "hearing-impaired" and chose not to be actively involved in the Deaf community.

I was dumbfounded at first, but soon realized that the deaf population throughout the world was more diverse than I ever imagined. I thought I had the answers for everyone, but soon found that what was a thrill for me might be a bitter pill for someone else. Despite the very real frustration of oral failures that I've described in this book, there *are* oralists out there who have succeeded at what they do. They're perfectly happy the way they are and have done very well for themselves, in situations that were unbearable for me.

One such oralist pointed out that if I preached my way as the answer for *all* deaf children, I was just as bad as the old-school teachers who forbid the use of sign language in their classrooms. Who was I to say my way was the only way? He had a good point. With that in mind, I took the notes of what eventually became the rough draft of this book and changed everything to an autobiographical format. Instead of a general book on deafness, I have instead chose the safer route of sharing my own personal experiences, and my conclusions related to them. You are, of course, free to draw your own conclusions and I encourage you to do so. If this book stirs just one healthy debate somewhere, I've done my job.

One day, I received e-mail from a woman who was tired of the same old oralist vs. ASL arguments that were all too common on deaf-l. She pointed out that many of the debates focused on oralists who preferred to be a part of the hearing world, and the culturally Deaf who advocated involvement in the Deaf world. Very nice, she said... but what about those who are stuck in between? Those who don't quite fit into the hearing world but also don't fit into the Deaf one? In other words, what about those who are "on the fence?"

She had me there. I hadn't really given it much thought lately, because over the years I've pretty much immersed myself into the Deaf world. Nonetheless, there was a time when I was still in limbo, caught between the Deaf and hearing worlds. I remembered how I wanted to attend PSD throughout my high school years, but instead had to remain at GFS. I remembered how initially, when I first got involved in the Deaf community, my signing was somewhat awkward. In fact, many Deaf people at both PSD and Gallaudet had remarked that I appeared to be "hearie-minded"; my signing ability and mannerisms were closer to what you would expect from a hearing person. It didn't matter. I plugged on. Based on my past experiences, I knew that I would never completely fit into the hearing world. Period. That's it, that's a hard-core fact that will never change. Sure, it's possible to assimilate into the hearing world with varying degrees of success (depending on residual hearing, speech, and lip-reading skills), but you can never fit in completely one hundred percent.

However, any deaf person, given a reasonable amount of time, can sufficiently learn how to use sign language. I did. And I gradually became a part of the Deaf world in a way I never could with the hearing world. To this day, I have never seen a deaf person learn how to hear and use that ability perfectly in the hearing world, yet I know of countless deaf people who found success and happiness in the Deaf world after years of struggling in the hearing one.

Granted, there are those who remain on the fence and simply don't feel a bond (or a need to bond) with the Deaf world. This is understandable. For example, during all those years at GFS, English and English alone was my primary language. ASL, as we all know, is a completely different language with a completely different syntax. So if you're joining the Deaf world late, it can be very frustrating because you are literally joining another culture... and it's nothing unusual to experience culture shock.

On many occasions in the Deaf world, I would sign (in English word order) a hearing idiom and be greeted with blank stares. Conversely, someone might throw me an ASL idiom, a sign or signed phrase that had no English equivalent, and I'd be confused. It took a while to adjust, and I can see why those who are on the fence might feel like they're in a completely different world. They are.

Is there any solution to this uncomfortable limbo of not quite fitting in here and not quite fitting in there? That depends on individual preference. As for me, I had two solutions that helped me adjust to the Deaf world.

Number one: find others who are going through the same thing you are. In other words, the best way for people on the fence to find comfort is to find other people who are on the fence! During my early years as an employee at PSD, as a student at Gallaudet and a member of a Deaf club, I found other deaf and hard of hearing people who were also relatively new to the scene. We had a lot in common and we were able to give each other a lot of support. In due time, we all became part of Deaf culture and I'm grateful for the experience.

Number two: find a mentor in the Deaf community. It helps to have a special friend who is culturally Deaf yet sensitive to your needs as a New Deafie. In my case, it was my friend Vijay who at the very last minute talked me out of leaving Gallaudet University in 1989. There were things going on at the University and in my personal life which were quite difficult for me at the time, and I might have given up on it were it not for Vijay. I might not be writing this book if it weren't for him.

Of course, I realize that my solutions do not apply to everyone; they are what worked very well for me. It must be acknowledged that there are still a lot of people who just don't feel comfortable in Deaf culture, and no one should force them to. In this case, the answer is similar to my first solution: find your peers, whoever they may be. If you consider yourself hard of hearing, if you don't really like signing that much... keep in mind that there are many deaf people who feel the same way. Find them. The worst thing about being on the fence, in my opinion, is the feeling that you are alone. Whoever you are and whatever you believe in, you can find your answers.

If you ask me what my own personal approach to deafness is, I offer three words: *go with deafness*. This coincides with a concept found in Tai Chi, another martial art I became involved with after moving back to Pennsylvania. One of the principles of Tai Chi is the fact that it's usually not recommended to go directly against an opponent's force. Instead, it is best to go *with* the energy, using an opponent's own force against him. When someone tries to push you, don't resist head-on; simply yield and turn in the direction you are being pushed. With just a little nudge, you can send your opponent flying off in that direction with the very energy he was trying to use on you.

Applying this to deafness, I found that it's similarly foolhardy for me to directly resist it. Just be deaf, I learned. Struggling against it and trying to be hearing (something I'll never be) goes against the flow, and it is incredibly exhausting. Why fight it? Rather than trying to fix myself into being the person other people wish I could be, I have found that things have worked best when I just focus on my positives and take it from there. I make the most of what I do have instead of wasting time on what I don't.

For some people, such a philosophy is incomprehensible. One such person wrote an article about this, which appeared in a Philadelphia newspaper. I found it quite perplexing. The author in question could not understand, in any way whatsoever, why so many deaf people were saying no to the cochlear implant. She could not understand why some of us don't want to be fixed. After all, she mused, the deaf must be missing out terribly on wonderful sounds such as birds singing, ocean waves crashing on the shore, and the wonders of music. In addition to that, this woman couldn't understand why Deaf people value sign language so much. She argued that sign language, for all its richness, has serious drawbacks. It's not possible to 'talk' in the dark, with your back to someone, or with your hands full, she surmised.

Although her concern was well-intentioned, it nonetheless overlooked the fact that what might be important to hearing people may not necessarily be important to deaf people. Instead of listening to Luciano Pavarotti with our ears, we can watch awe-inspiring Deaf Poet/Storyteller Peter Cook with our eyes. Although there are deaf people out there who can and do enjoy music (either through residual hearing or feeling the vibrations), it's not that big a deal. Truth is, there are *several* ways to find spiritual enjoyment. For some, it may be hiking through a nature area. For others, it could be mountain climbing, reading a great book, painting, and many other examples. For me, walking at night along a moonlit beach is inspiring. Do you see me writing an article saying that people in Kansas are spiritually deprived because they don't live anywhere near a beach? Of course not. There are countless wonders in this world, and countless ways to enjoy them.

As for the comments about sign language drawbacks, it needs to be pointed out that everything has advantages and disadvantages. Sure, I can't sign in the dark, but how about those loud nightclubs and other places where hearing people have to shout into each other's ears? Deaf people in such noisy environments sign to each other conveniently without any problem, even across the room if necessary.

As for not being able to sign with your hands full... is there anything more disgusting than verbally talking with your *mouth* full? Give me a break. Pure and simple, different people have different abilities. Let us enjoy what we can, and don't worry about what we can't. I feel we're

189

better off celebrating our differences instead of imposing our values onto each other.

Basically, I recognize that no two deaf people are alike and that each person has a right to their individuality. If you're deaf, and you're comfortable being deaf the way that only *you* can be deaf, then more power to you. Whether you consider yourself capital-D Deaf or hard of hearing, that's something only you can decide for yourself. I personally don't think any two deaf people are exactly alike. For example, I can enjoy music, and I can recognize certain songs by certain artists. I can even learn the words to some of those songs. However, I can't speak with hearing people on the phone by voice, no matter how hard I try (I need to use the TDD relay services, like most deaf people). Meanwhile, my old roommate Jeff is the exact opposite: as far as music goes, he can't recognize any songs by any particular artists. Yet somehow, he can speak on the phone by voice with his hearing relatives. Hey, it's an ability he has, good for him. It was interesting to see these differences in each other, which were so pronounced that we would jokingly accuse each other of being hearing. Regardless, we both consider each other culturally Deaf.

So... is there a specific look we're supposed to have, a specific way we're supposed to act? I don't think so. We all have the right to be individuals. If a deaf person accuses me of brownnosing with hearing people when I use my voice (yes, it's happened), I shrug it off. I'm only taking advantage of an ability I have. What's wrong with using it? On the other hand, if someone tries promoting exclusive oralism for prelingually deaf children, I often speak up for the virtues of sign language. I have done so many times in debates that have raged on deaf-l, with varying levels of support and disagreement from other participants.

So what's the answer, really? The closest thing I could find came from one of the more level-headed members of deaf-l. After much haggling over this communication philosophy and that communication philosophy, this education style and that education style, a Chris deHahn mercifully intervened with a classic posting. With his permission, I offer you his original note as it came out in April 1995:

The cure for deafness is our deaf children.

Sometimes I think we spend so much time theorizing, studying, working toward our methodologies that we forget why we're doing it and who we're doing it for. It doesn't matter what methodology we choose. What matters is that we teach our children to be open minded and objective. We need to focus on their abilities, instead of their disability. If a child is a beautiful signer, we need to praise him or her. If a child has beautiful speech, we need to praise him or her. If a student does well in class, we need to praise him or her. We must teach our children tolerance of others' beliefs. We do this best by example.

Tolerance and understanding are the best lessons we can teach our children. It's so much more important than sign language linguistics or proper oral pronunciation.

There is a cure for deafness. We can cure it by showing the world our children and their accomplishments. We can show the world a world of deaf children that can communicate differently, yet they all respect each other for their differences. We can show our politicians, our business leaders, our community leaders, that our children are different yet they are capable of anything. Our children will break down the barriers of deafness. We owe them our patience, our respect, and our help.

Amen, Chris, Amen. This is the closest I have ever seen anyone come to a solution to deafness that applies to everyone. When parents and professionals look for "the answer" to deafness, they invariably wind up arguing over communication methodologies. Although for me, ASL has been a godsend, I can't preach it for everyone. However, if people are willing to put aside their strong opinions about this communication method or that communication method, I do believe I have a general formula which guarantees success for the most deaf children. It is quite simple, really. Deaf children need:

1) Loving, supportive parents
2) A communication system which is effective for them
3) A good school with full accessibility
4) Consistent parental involvement at school and at home
5) Successful Deaf role models
6) High expectations... from both parents and teachers
7) Lots of reading and writing
8) More reading and writing
9) Repeat 7, 8, and 9 as necessary

If it looks like I've put considerable emphasis on the parents... well... exactly! For virtually all kids, deaf or hearing, it has almost always been parental support that has enabled them to conquer the many challenges they face while growing up. To just be involved, to provide a loving environment, and to encourage achievement is almost always enough. My own parents, and especially my grandparents, didn't always know the answers to dealing with a deaf child, but they were always there... and in the long run, that was more than enough for me.

Chapter 11

Eventually, Melanie and I found a nice townhouse in North Wales, Pennsylvania. Melanie earned her Master's degree in Deaf Education and has been teaching for a few years, doing a fantastic job. But the biggest event of them all came on January 21, 1999 – when our beautiful son, Darren Michael Drolsbaugh, was born.

It is here where things have come full circle, in an incredibly positive way. Whereas this book opened with my own birth, a veritable horror story, this one shows how accessibility has greatly improved. For when Darren was born, my wife and I were fully involved throughout the whole process.

As we checked into Warminster Hospital, a phone with a TTY was provided. The hospital had also arranged for two interpreters, who took shifts while Melanie went through labor, childbirth and follow-up medical care afterwards. Melanie and I had not bothered with any of the Lamaze classes that many couples take, figuring it was all hooey anyway (we knew that at the first hint of pain, Melanie was going to scream for epidural).

Nonetheless, during the actual birth, the nurse gave specific breathing instructions, instructions that helped immensely... instructions that would have gone completely over our heads had there not been an interpreter. It was an absolute godsend and we welcomed our son into this world with much joy.

Shortly after Darren was born, the popular television show *ER* came on... which we could watch if we wanted to, because the hospital also provided captioned TV. But no, I had seen enough gory stuff for one day, and turned the TV off. But the bottom line, though, is obvious: TTYs, interpreters, captioned TV, you name it, we had everything. Compare that to my own birth in 1966, when my parents were left in the dark, and you can see how we've come a long way. And of course, above all, the most important thing is that we left the hospital with the biggest bundle of joy one could ever ask for.

Inevitably, people wind up asking the same question over and over: *is Darren deaf or hearing?* Not that I care, because Darren is Darren and we love him immensely regardless of his hearing status. But for now, all indications point towards the fact that he is hearing. Perhaps he will remain hearing and someday write a book titled *Hearing Again*. Or maybe he will follow the same pattern my father and I did, losing hearing later in life (in which case he could write *Deaf Again: The Next Generation*). Know what? It doesn't really matter. So long as he's happy, I'm happy.

Although Darren was born into Deaf culture and will always be a part of it regardless of his hearing ability, I do recognize that he is still a hearing person. While he is being exposed to sign language – he's already signing "daddy," "milk," "cat," and "bye-bye" – I understand that he needs to interact with other hearing people. I have seen the value of this at his daycare center. We've noticed that by socializing with his hearing peers, Darren has picked up some things that he otherwise would have missed at home.

For example, after a few weeks in daycare, Darren has developed an appreciation for music. He loves listening to people singing songs, and he even does this cute little bouncy dance. And one day after we brought him home from daycare, he spontaneously began clapping his hands. We knew this was something he picked up from hearing culture; after all, we do the "Deaf applause" hand-wave at home.

Ultimately, we believe that it is Darren's right as a hearing person to be exposed to hearing peers and role models, even though he's growing up in a primarily Deaf environment. We know he will make the best of both worlds, and want him to have the opportunity to learn from each one.

And yes, you probably see where this is going... I want to point out that likewise, it is only fair that deaf children get the opportunity to interact with deaf peers and role models. It would be unfair if I kept Darren separated from other hearing people, and I hope people can understand that it would be equally unfair to keep deaf children separated from the Deaf community.

From time to time, I have heard hearing parents express fear that the Deaf community would "steal" their deaf children away from them. This has puzzled me in the past, and now that I have a child of my own, it puzzles me even more. After all, I do not fear that hearing culture will "steal" my hearing son from me. Quite the contrary, I welcome hearing relatives, teachers and peers into his life so that he can have all the more enriching experiences. We all deserve the opportunity to find out who we are...and as you can see in this book, it was such an opportunity that turned my life around.

Often, when people ask me what the turning point in my life was, I tell them about Linda Baine pulling me out of the supermarket and eventually helping me discover something which is known as Deaf Pride. Many people simply do not understand this phenomenon. After all, they ask, how could someone possibly be *proud* of what in essence is nothing more than a disability? On top of that, deafness is a disability that affects communication... it can put an invisible wall between hearing and deaf people. So what's there to be proud of?

If you had asked me this question many years ago, I would have been hard-pressed to come up with an answer. Deaf Pride? What Deaf Pride? What about all those times in hearing schools when I had to give up and simply say "I don't know" because I couldn't understand the teacher? What about all those times I was made fun of? What about all those times I was put in an audiologist's booth like a guinea pig? What about all those times speech teachers squeezed my mouth and said, "c'mon, can you say BA-BA-BA?" Certainly nothing to be proud of. In fact, I was downright *embarrassed* at times.

That is, I was embarrassed until I got to join Deaf culture. I may have joined it late, after years of unsuccessfully trying to be like a hearing person, but better late than never. Meeting other deaf peers like myself, sharing similar stories of oppression and ridicule, learning ASL, and seeing other deaf adults succeed has completely changed my attitude. I am no longer ashamed of my deafness, I am proud of it. I am proud of who I am, proud of what I've overcome, and proud of my culture.

Yes, I recognize such a thing as Deaf culture. Some people may be sighing, "oh no, not that old culture vs. pathology argument." I acknowledge that there are many people out there, even deaf people, who insist that deafness is nothing more than an annoying disability. As my past would indicate, that could certainly be an accurate description. Other people adamantly insist that there is a Deaf culture (emphasizing the capital D), that deafness is not a handicap at all, that "Deaf people can do anything but hear."

I choose to take somewhat of a middle stance. My own definition is that *deafness is a disability that is so unique, its very nature causes a culture to emerge from it.* Participation in this culture is voluntary… and I officially enlisted in 1989.

Being a part of this culture has given me a sense of pride. I am no longer alone. I share a language, ASL, with many other people in the Deaf community. I share a history of struggle that is well-documented; not only there are stories related to growing up deaf passed along within the Deaf community, but there are now countless books as well. I enjoy ASL poetry and Deaf puns/jokes that cannot be translated into written English; they are unique in that they can only be understood within the framework of ASL. I enjoy attending plays and community events that focus on many Deaf issues. I also use a number of Deaf mannerisms, of which there are several. The "Deaf applause" cheer (waving one's hands in the air instead of clapping), a repertoire of visual expressions and signs that relay concepts far quicker than mere words ever could, and a tendency to be more physically-oriented (i.e. tapping my foot, tapping someone's shoulder, waving, blinking lights, etc., to get someone's attention), and so on.

Last but not least, I bask in pride when I see Deaf people becoming more and more successful in the world. There are those who feel that Deaf culture shelters Deaf people from the "real world", but from my perspective, it *strengthens* us and enables us to make the most of both worlds. Participating in a core group such as the Deaf community, in my opinion, provides a strong foundation of inner strength and self-esteem that helps people succeed anywhere they want to, including the mainstream. This is, after all, what the whole book is about.

Indeed, more and more Deaf people are getting advanced degrees and becoming doctors, lawyers, administrators, and (ahem) authors. It is a feeling of pride and support that pushes us on. In my case, it was seeing the successful outcome of the Deaf President Now movement that spurred me on to transfer to Gallaudet

University and set my goals higher than I ever did before. What really sticks out in my mind is that ten years ago, I never would have thought that any of this would be possible. As the pseudo-hearing child I was so many years ago, I had grown accustomed to depending on other people, being lost in the crowd, and accepting limits that others imposed on me (as well as some that I imposed on myself). Today, however, I stand on my own two feet. So yes, as far as I'm concerned, there is such a thing as Deaf Pride. It exists for me, and it's the spark that changed my life. As one would say in ASL, "Deaf Pride, Pah!"

Epilogue

When I first wrote and published *Deaf Again* in 1997, it was one of the hardest things I ever did in my life. Normally, writing a book and having it published is the thrill of a lifetime. But this book was a bit too personal. This was about my family, all the good stuff and the bad stuff. Mostly good stuff, but... the bad stuff was brutally honest. Like many other deaf people with hearing relatives, I have experienced a considerable number of communication difficulties.

It can be a real bummer, something every family with a deaf child should be aware of. And for the deaf children themselves, I wanted to provide something they could relate to – an opportunity to show family and friends this book, an opportunity to say "see, that's exactly how I felt." Incidentally, that is precisely what has happened, and I'm happy with the results. However...

When the very first shipment of books were fresh off the press, I nearly stopped in my tracks. I couldn't go through with it. Every worse-case scenario flashed through my mind. My family was either going to have their feelings hurt, or they were going to be mad as hell. Or both. They would disown me and I would move to a remote cabin somewhere in Switzerland.

After much soul-searching, I decided to go for it with *Deaf Again*. If I was guilty of anything, it was of telling the truth... truth that needed to be heard. My biggest reinforcement came from Lisa Bain, an accomplished writer who has published three books of her own. When I expressed my concern about family members feeling bad about certain deaf issues, she smiled knowingly. Then in her own polite, thoughtful way, she asked:

"Don't you think they already know?"

She was right. Yes, they already knew. It was never an issue of knowing about deafness; it was about coping with it. There were no answers for my family until they read the book. Immediately, the changes were obvious.

During a small get-together with some hearing friends and relatives, my hearing grandmother caught me struggling in a conversation with someone. She saw me staring intently at the person's lips, straining my neck, asking the person to repeat a few things, and finally just nodding it off when it got too frustrating. Grandmom turned to my mother and said,

"He doesn't understand a word, does he?"

At last! She always knew... but today, she *understood*. So much, in fact, that at the next major family gathering, she agreed to make arrangements for a sign language interpreter. Pah! What followed was a major breakthrough.

Three weeks later, there we all were. Several hearing relatives, three Deaf people (my mother, my wife and myself) and one very competent interpreter. It was nirvana. Dinner table conversation was no longer a bore. Grandmom was telling a story about how her mother used to keep live fish in the bathtub before preparing them for dinner. My uncle and two other relatives were having a heavy debate about religious pluralism. I watched with fascination. A whole new world had opened. These strangers at the dinner table had suddenly transformed into very interesting people!

It didn't matter if the Deaf relatives were actively involved in the conversation or not. Sometimes we joined in; sometimes we just sat back and enjoyed the show. With the interpreter, we had a new set of ears which let us know what was going on at all times. There was no boredom whatsoever.

The real kicker was a conversation with my cousin Eleanor. A pleasant young woman, Eleanor has always been an interesting person. However, her speech pattern for whatever reason has always been difficult for me to follow. I never realized it until just then, but I had always manipulated our conversations in such a way that it never went beyond the superficial. For if we had ever jumped to a brand new topic, I would not have been able to keep up. It's much easier to lip-read when you know the conversation will stick to "how's the family" and "how's the job."

With the interpreter, though, we took it to a new level. During the discussion on religious issues, I was surprised to find myself agreeing with Eleanor several times. From a philosophical standpoint, we were practically twins. Only then, after all these years, did I realize this. To top it off, I also discovered she takes an Aikido class and shares a similar interest in the martial arts. I have been a martial artist for several years, most recently becoming involved in Tai Chi, yet I had never had such a discussion with Eleanor. I had no idea she was into the same thing. We wound up having a great talk, sharing notes about our respective martial arts styles. All of this thanks to the 'terp.

When the evening drew to a close, I checked my watch and did a double-take. It was 10:30 p.m. Under the usual circumstances (no interpreter and plenty of boredom), I would have been out of there by 7:30. This time, however, I stayed for the whole duration and got to know my family on a different level. So... looking back on *Deaf Again*... yes, it was *deafinitely* worth it.

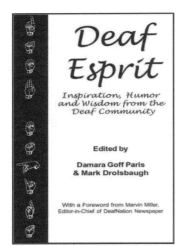

Introducing a new book from the author of *Deaf Again!*

Imagine being Deaf and living through the German occupation of Norway during World War II.

Learn about life among the Deaf Navajos.

Find out how a Deaf boy creates an ASL version of Rock-Scissors-Paper.

Experience Deaf pride in the late 60's.

Agonize with a mother as she tries to make sense of the Cochlear Implant controversy.

Laugh in the library with well-known comedian CJ Jones.

Penned by twenty-five contributors from all walks of life within the Deaf Community, **Deaf Esprit: Inspiration, Humor and Wisdom from the Deaf Community**, edited by Damara Goff Paris and Mark Drolsbaugh, is a compilation of stories that will provoke a smile, a tear, and most importantly, a sense of well-being. Aptly named after the expression "*esprit de corps*," *Deaf Esprit* brings about the power of the spirit of the Deaf Community.

AGO Gifts and Publications
ORDER FORM

Name: _____

Address: _____

City: _____

State: _____ Zip: _____

Payment Method:

_____Check/Money Order _____Visa _____Mastercard

Card Number: _____

Expiration Date: _____

Signature (required):_____

Date of Order: _____

Order Information:

_____ "Deaf Esprit" at $14.95 each for a total of: _____

Shipping and Handling: _____

TOTAL: _____

Shipping and Handling Rates:
1–5 books: $4.95   6–10 books: $6.95
11–20 books: $9.95   21–50 books: $12.95
*Over 50 books, contact for rates

Mail all orders to: **AGO Gifts and Publications**
                                    P.O. Box 17664
                                    Salem, Oregon 97305

Credit Card Orders may be faxed to: (503) 304-1961